New And Improved Bartender's Manual: Or How To Mix Drinks Of The Present Style

Harry Johnson

NEW AND IMPROVED

—✳ ILLUSTRATED ✳—

BARTENDER'S * MANUAL

—• OR: •—

HOW TO MIX DRINKS

—• OF THE •—

PRESENT STYLE,

NTAINING A VALUABLE LIST OF INSTRUCTIONS AND HINTS BY THE
AUTHOR IN REFERENCE TO ATTENDING A BAR; ALSO A LARGE LIST
OF MIXED DRINKS, SUCH AS AMERICAN, BRITISH, FRENCH,
GERMAN, ITALIAN, RUSSIAN, SPANISH, ETC., ETC., WITH
ILLUSTRATIONS, AND A COMPLETE LIST OF BAR
UTENSILS, WINES, LIQUORS, ALES, MIXTURES,
ETC., ETC.

HARRY JOHNSON,

BLISHER AND PROFESSIONAL BARTENDER,

——AND——

INSTRUCTOR IN THE ART HOW TO ATTEND A BAR,

NEW YORK CITY.

641.97

J67n

Harry Johnson

PREFACE BY THE PUBLISHER OF THE NEW AND IMPROVED ILLUSTRATED BARKEEPER'S MANUAL.

In presenting this manual to the public, I beg the indulgence for making a few remarks in regard to myself. Having been in the Hotel and Liquor business in various capacities since my boyhood, I was enabled to study its practice and management in regard to drinks, etc., and having travelled all over this and other countries in order to learn and obtain the different styles of mixed drinks, I have after careful preparation, time and expense succeeded in compiling this work and I challenge any party to criticise it and find one recipe which is not fully and completely prepared. This work is written in a very plain language, so as to have it useful for everyone; I have always been employed in some of the most prominent, leading and first-class Hotels and Barrooms, in this city as well as in other large cities, and in all parts of the United States and other countries, from all of which I have the very highest letters of recommendation as to my complete knowledge and ability in managing a Barroom or Hotel, etc., and in preparing and mixing drinks of every kind and form in the latest style. I have described and illustrated in a plain, straightforward manner, that is understood all over the world all the popular Mixed Drinks, Cocktails, Punches, Juleps and other fancy drinks, etc., etc. In addition this book will give you an entire and complete list of instructions, to be observed in attending a bar, in conducting yourself, in opening a Saloon in the morning, how to serve and wait on customers, and all the various details connected with the business, so that any person who contemplates entering the business of a bartender, has a complete and valuable guide, and illustrations to guide him. In this work you will also find a complete list of all the bar utensils, as well as a complete list of Liquors, Glass- and Silverware, Mixtures, etc., that you require, and the different brands of beverages you will need, and how to use them. Also a large number of valuable hints and information to bartenders, in what manner to compile them, and in fact every item that is of any use whatever from the moment you become a bartender, to the requirements of each day. Even people thoroughly experienced and competent in this business, will find this book, after a careful examination, to be as handy to them as to any new beginner. I have also made it my profession for many years back to teach the art of attending a bar to any party having an inclination to learn; in past years I have taught a great number of parties the profession in the latest style and in the most scientific manner, and I can with pride refer to them as to my fitness as an instructor of bartending. In conclusion let me say, that this work will not only be very valuable to the entire profession it is intended for, but will prove to be of great advantage to all families and the public in general, as a complete guide in preparing and teaching the art of mixing drinks and attending a bar.

Furthermore, as to the style and the art of mixing (see illustrations, plates 1 and 3), this work will contain nothing but the most respectable reading matter. I remain,

Your obedient servant,

HARRY JOHNSON.

INDEX.

RULES AND REGULATIONS.

FROM 1 TO 43.

LIST OF UTENSILS, WINES, LIQUORS, Etc.

FROM 44 TO 55.

LIST OF MIXED DRINKS.

FROM 56 TO 242.

PLATE No. 1.

HARRY JOHNSON'S STYLE OF MIXING DRINKS TO A PARTY OF SIX.
Copyrighted, 1888.

1. HOW TO ATTEND A BAR;

the general appearance of the bartender, and how he should conduct himself at all times when on duty, etc.

THE author of this work has after careful deliberation compiled the following rules for the proper management of a saloon, and would suggest the following instructions in regard to attending a bar. He has endeavored, to the best of his ability, to state them in perfectly plain and straightforward language, as it must be conducted in a systematic and proper manner, the same as any other business. When waiting on customers at any time, it is of the highest importance for a bartender to be strictly polite and attentive in his behavior, and especially in his manner of speech, giving prompt answers to all questions as far as lies in his power; he should be cheerful, and have a bright and pleasant countenance. It is of very great importance to be neat, clean, and tidy in dress, as that will prove more to the interest of the bartender than any other matter; he should be pleasant and cheerful with everyone; this will not only be pleasing to customers but also prove advantageous to the bartender serving them. It is proper, when a person steps up to the bar, for a bartender to set before him a glass of ice-water, and then in a genteel and polite manner find out what he may desire. If mixed drinks should be called for, it is the bartender's duty to mix and prepare them above the counter, and let the customers or parties see them, and they should be prepared in such a neat, quick and scientific way, as to draw attention; it is also the bartender's duty to see to it that everything used with the drinks is perfectly clean, and the glasses bright and polished. .When the customer has finished and left the bar, the bartender should clean the counter, well and thoroughly, so that it will have a neat and good appearance again, and if time should allow the bartender to do so, he should clean the glasses used in a perfect manner at once, so as to have them ready again when needed; as regards the bench, which is an important branch in managing a bar properly, it is the bartenders special duty to have his bench cleared up and in good shape at all times, he will find it to his advantage, if done properly. (See illustration, plate No. 2). Other particular points are the style, and the saving of time. Whenever you have to mix drinks which require to be strained into a separate fancy glass, such as Cocktails, Sours, Fizz's, etc., to make it a rule to place the glass of ice-water in front of the customer, next to it the glass into which you intend to strain the drink, and then go to work and mix the drink required; try to place your glassware on the counter all in one row or straight line. As to the style of the bartender, it is proper that when on duty, or while mixing drinks that he should stand straight, carry his head erect and place himself in a fine position. (See illustrations, plates 1 and 3.)

2. HINTS ABOUT TRAINING A BOY TO THE BUSINESS.

For the last thirty years of my experience, I had the opportunity of training hundreds and hundreds of boys into our trade, and I would suggest to any proprietor, manager or bartender to treat the boy strictly, teaching him manners, and see that he does not become impudent to you or to customers. I would advise the man behind the Bar to give him all the particular points and information regarding the business, talk to him in a pleasant but still commanding way, and don't let him hear bad language, if you can help it, see to it that he always looks neat and have him obey your orders in every shape and form. Meanwhile give him the liberty that belongs to him, and by doing so, you will turn out a very smart, good and useful boy, fit for your business, and whenever you have the opportunity, it is your duty to set a good example to the boy; teach him as much as you are able, so that when he becomes a man, he can call himself a gentleman, and need not be ashamed of his business.

A good many people, I am sorry to say, are laboring under the impression that there is no such thing as a gentleman in the Liquor business. If those people, however, knew the inside of our business thoroughly, or became acquainted with some good man employed therein, they soon would come to the conclusion that none but gentlemen could carry on the Liquor business in a strict and systematic way. The great trouble is, that most of these narrow-minded people don't know much about anything and consequently are led to place all men in our business under the same heading

3. HINTS FROM THE AUTHOR.

The author of this work would like to make a few remarks in regard to an important branch which has been greatly neglected. Wherever you go or whatever saloon you visit, you will find, with but few exceptions, no matter how elegantly the place is furnished or fitted up, the bench usually constructed in a very mean and ill-shaped way. Now the remedy I would recommend is, that whenever a party has a saloon or barroom fitted up, not to leave all the arrangements to the cabinetmaker, but make it a special point to have the bench constructed in a comfortable and neat manner, so that it will show off and be handy at the same time, especially in regard to ice and water boxes, etc.; also have them large and convenient enough, so that bottles can be placed between the bench and the top of the counter. Have the sugar box or bowl, etc., arranged so that it is in convenient reach for you, thus losing neither time nor steps. It is, furthermore, of importance, that the boxes containing the water are always kept perfectly clean, so that in case any of your customers steps or looks behind the bar, he will find it so, and, really, I think it should be the pride of any bartender, to show his boss as well as his customers in what good condition he keeps his bench. The floor behind the bar should also look clean and perfectly dry, so that both, bench and floor, will give full satisfaction to the proprietor as well as to the public, and not alone that, but it will also be beneficial to the health of the man doing the work behind the bar. (See illustration, plate 2.)

4. TREATMENT OF PATRONS—BEHAVIOR TOWARDS THEM.

The first rule to be observed by any man acting as bartender in our business, is to treat all customers with the utmost politeness and respect. It is also a very important matter, to serve the customers with the very best of liquors, wines, beer, cigars, etc., that can be had for the money; in this, of course, one must be governed by the style of house he keeps and the prices charged. Show to your patrons that you are a man of business and endeavor to do only what is right and just, by refusing to sell anything either to intoxicated or disorderly persons, or to minors. The customer will then respect you as a gentleman and a business man. No man employed in our business should make distinctions between customers on account of their appearance. As long as they behave as gentlemen, they should be treated as such, no matter what business they may pursue. Therefore all the customers, whether rich or poor, should be served alike, not only in the same respectful manner, but with the same quality of goods; not keeping a separate bottle for rich people and an inferior grade for poorer people, unless you have a customer before you who prefers quantity to quality. In observing these rules you will build up a reputation as a first-class business man who carries on his business in accordance with business principles, and will find it safe and easy to succeed. But there is a way of spoiling your customers, and that is by offering too much, or *treating* too often. This is especially the case with many people, on opening a new place of business. It is always the wisest to give your customers all they are entitled to, but no more.

5. RULES FOR BARTENDERS
to be observed in entering on and going off duty.

When the stipulated time arrives for a bartender to quit, it is his duty to see to it, that his bench is in perfect order, that all his bottles are filled, his ice box has sufficient ice in it, that all glassware is clean, and everything straightened out in such a manner, that when his relief arrives, he will have no difficulty and can immediately commence to serve customers. When the relief takes charge, it is his duty to convince himself, that nothing has been neglected and everything is properly arranged to enable him to perform his duty satisfactorily. Where there is no check system, the cash must be properly arranged as well as everything else. This is generally done by the proprietor, or the one having the management of the business, so that there will be no difficulty in regard to the cash, which is the most important point in business.

6. RULES IN REFERENCE TO A "GIGGER."

In all my recipes for the various drinks, you will find the word "Wine Glass" as the article to be used in which to mix the drinks. The wine glass is only used for compiling those recipes; but for measuring the mixture, etc., the proper article to be used is what we call a "gigger," otherwise considerable liquor would be wasted, in case of a rush; it will also enable you to get your drinks at once, the way the customers desire to have them, either strong or medium, by using a "gigger," as there is no man in the business who can pour out of a bottle a certain quantity of liquor by guessing at it, especially when the bottles used are only half filled or nearly empty. The "gigger" is of silver-plated metal and is shaped like a sherry glass without the long stem; it is durable and almost impossible to break; it is used by all first-class bartenders, excepting only a few experts in mixing drinks, who have such practice and experience, that they can measure without "gigger" or even a glass.

7. THE OPENING OF A NEW PLACE.

The most important thing to be looked after in opening a new place is its location. The more prominently the business is located the more benefit you will derive from it, and the easier it will be for you to obtain customers. The next in order is the laying out of the store, as regards fixtures, such as counter, back bar, ice-box, liquor cases, closets, and everything belonging to it; because in selecting the right kind of fixtures, that will fit the place nicely, you will give it a good appearance, instead of overcrowding it or having it look bare and empty.

My advice to any one starting a new place, is to consider well the location, and then obtain a lease, sufficiently long to make him safe on that score; then the running expenses, such as rent, wages, gas, ice, lunch, etc., must be calculated, and if the investment is not too large, and the necessary expenses compare favorably with the amount of business expected, it is likely to be a successful undertaking, provided the starter has the necessary knowledge and confidence in his ability to carry on and manage a business on strict business principles as it should be managed. But after all these considerations, and before contracting any obligations, even before signing a lease, you must have the assurance of obtaining a license.

8. FIRST DUTY IN OPENING A BAR ROOM IN THE MORNING.

The greatest attraction of a barroom is the appearance of it. Now, the first thing a bartender must do after opening the saloon in the morning, is to give the place a perfect ventilation; after this is accomplished, prepare your ice water, so as to be ready in case it is demanded. Then turn your attention to the bottles containing liquors, mixtures, etc., and see that they are filled and corked; place those that require it on ice; when that is finished have your porter to clean the floor properly and then dust all the wood work, clean and polish the windows, mirrors, etc.; then go to work on your bench, place all the glassware on top of the counter, but using as little space as is consistent, so in case you have customers during that time you have plenty of room to wait upon them; next give the bench a perfect scrubbing or washing; then wash your glassware well in clean water, and place those that belong there back on the bench; then see that the bar and ice boxes are filled up with fine shaved ice. After having your bar and all other bottles, well cleaned and polished, see to it that your wines and liquors are nice, cool, pleasant and in proper condition. Also cut up your fruits, that will be required during the day, such as oranges, pineapples, berries, and cocktail peels. See that your roller towels and napkins are perfectly clean, and changed as often as it becomes necessary, and have everything handy for business. Furthermore I would recommend to any bartender to have this part of the work done as quickly as possible, and try to make his own appearance behind the bar, as neat and clean as he can, as soon as the work permits him to do so, and not stand behind the bar, like a great many bartenders which I have seen, and I am sorry to say it, in their shirt sleeves the greater part of the forenoon, looking mean enough to drive out the customers.

I would also like to call the attention to one particular thing, namely the water glasses filled with ice water. In my experience I have often seen bartenders being neglectful as to water glasses. It is proper in placing them in front of the customer, to see to it that they are clean and perfectly filled up, because this will cover up the marks, left by the previous customer, but the most proper way is to hand out a clean empty water tumbler, and hand a pitcher of ice water for the customer to help himself. This is well worth remembering.

9. THE PROPER STYLE IN OPENING AND SERVING CHAMPAGNES.

In serving champagne, the bartender, after being informed what brand the customer requires, takes the bottle from the ice, twists or cuts off the wire, and then cuts the string by which the cork is held in place, just below the neck of the bottle; if cut otherwise, parts of the string, with some of the sealing wax attached to it, will remain fastened to the bottle, and particles of wax are liable to drop into the glass while pouring out the wine. After the cork is removed, the mouth and neck of the bottle should be wiped off with a clean towel or napkin. When a party of gentlemen come into your place of business, and wine is called for, place the glasses before them, and as a matter of politeness first pour a few drops into the glass of the gentlemen who called for the wine, then fill the glasses of those he invited before filling up his own glass. This rule of etiquette should be observed in serving any

PLATE No. 2,

This Illustration shows how to keep your working-bench in condition. Copyrighted, 1885.

wine, whether champagne or not. If a party calls for champagne at the table, place the bottle in an ice cooler; it is also not proper to uncork the bottle previous to placing it upon the table before the guests. If frozen champagne, which is often called for, is desired, place the bottle in the ice cooler and then fill up the cooler with broken ice and rock salt to the top, then revolve the bottle backward and forward with both hands as rapidly as possible; then cut the string and draw the cork and place a clean napkin over the mouth of the bottle; you will find that the wine will freeze much quicker in this way than if leaving the cork in the bottle. This is what is called frozen wine or champagne *frappé*.

10. A FEW WORDS IN REGARD TO LAGER BEER.

The above drink is so well known in this country as well as in all parts of the world, that only a few remarks are necessary about it. But I will here mention, that it requires the same attention as all the other liquors or beverages, and even more than some of them. It depends entirely on the manner of handling it, whether beer has a nice, refreshing taste or not. It should always be kept at an even temperature, according to the atmosphere and season of the year. In summer at a temperature of from 40 to 45 degrees, and should be kept at least three or four days in the ice house before tapping it. I would therefore advise anyone wishing to sell lager beer in his place of business, not to spare the expense of having an A No. 1 ice box or ice house, and keep it always in good working condition, by having it filled up with ice sufficiently to obtain the required temperature in all seasons of the year. Have the ice box or ice house large enough for the demands of your business, and you will at all times have good lager beer without trouble.

11. HOW LAGER BEER SHOULD BE DRAWN AND SERVED.

The proper way to draw lager beer, is directly from the keg, not using the first one or two glasses drawn, until the beer runs freely; then the vent must be knocked into the bung. If lager beer is drawn through pipes, these must be made of the very best material, which in this case would be English block tin, and be kept perfectly clean and in good order. It is customary to have an air or water pressure constantly acting upon the beer, when it is drawn through pipes, to prevent it from getting flat or stale, and impart a fresh and pleasant taste to the beer. But proper attention must be given to keeping the boiler containing the air in a very clean condition, and if the boiler should stand in a place where the air is impure, it is advisable to connect the boiler and pump by means of a pipe with a place where perfectly pure and fresh air is obtainable, as foul air would give the beer a bad taste and is liable to sicken the people drinking it. The beer remaining in the pipes over night should not be used. Attention must be given, that the pressure on the beer is not too high, as this would prevent it from running freely through the pipes, and by turning it into froth or cream, make it unhandy for the bartender to draw; there is also danger of an explosion, if the pressure gets very high, and this might destroy the beer kegs, pipes or the rubber hose connections with the boiler; an explosion is more likely to occur at night than during the day. Before drawing lager beer, the bartender must see to it, that the glasses are perfectly clean; after filling the glasses, remove the superfluous froth with a little ruler; by doing this you will prevent a great deal of moisture from spreading over the counter and floor, besides the foam in the glass will remain firm longer, and so prevent the beer from getting flat as quickly; by not removing the loose froth with a ruler, the air bubbles on top will sink through the froth and dissolve it. When a customer orders a second glass of beer, the same glass should be filled out of which he drank before, without previous rinsing, because the beer will thus taste and look better, and your customer will be more satisfied. If a party of two or more are standing up to the bar, and a second round is called for, it is proper to take the same glasses, one by one, and fill them, not taking two or three glasses at a time, as a great many bartenders do, for they as well as the customers are liable to mix the glasses, which is not very pleasant to the customers. Handling the glasses carefully is pleasing to the customers and should be done, if the bartender has sufficient time to do it, but in case of a rush, put the glasses used in the first round aside and let the customer see that you take fresh glasses for each round. The same is to be observed in serving customers sitting around a table. These rules are of importance in drawing and serving lager beer, and will please the customers if properly carried out. See to it that your beer is always cold enough in summer, and has the right temperature in winter. During the very hot season the temperature of the beer should be between 40 and 45 degrees.

12. ABOUT BOTTLED LAGER BEER.
(Imported as well as Domestic.)

With bottled lager beer this is altogether different. It must not be kept on ice, but in a very cool place in the ice box, in a standing position to allow the sediment to settle. In pouring the beer from the bottles, it is the bartenders duty to select a proper and clean glass. These rules should be observed with imported as well as with domestic beer.

13. ABOUT CLEANING BEER AND ALE PIPES.

At present nearly every saloon having either lager-beer, ale, or porter, so called malt liquors on tap, is supplied with an apparatus, and the boiler, pipes, rubber hose and other attachments to it must be kept perfectly clean. This will be easy to accomplish in the following manner: If a barrel of beer or ale is emptied and it is found necessary to cleanse the pipes, take a pail or two of hot water, and stir into it about $1/2$ pound of washing soda, put this fluid into the empty barrel, attach the vent and put on the pressure, then turn on the faucet and let it take its own course, the same as beer, and it will be forced through the pipes. When you notice that the barrel is emptied, take out the vent and pour in a few pailfuls of clean water; then close the vent and again put on the pressure to force the clean water trough the pipes. You will find that in this way all the pipes and connections can be easely and perfectly cleaned, and will smell fresh, and you are sure of having good beer. More or less time may elapse before a cleaning becomes necessary, but it is generally safe to have it performed once or twice a week, according to the amount of business done.

14. HOW TO IMPROVE THE APPEARANCE OF BAR AND TOILET ROOMS.

It is the duty of a bartender to keep everything connected with the barroom in the cleanest possible manner, so that it will attract the attention and admiration of customers and visitors. This will also aid in preserving the pictures and other ornaments. Have the fixtures, oiled up occasionally, using good and clean linseed oil, and not to much of it; woodwork should be thoroughly cleaned before putting on the oil. I have often been in places where they lavish all their attention on one particular thing, to the detriment of all others, and especially the toilet room, which in my opinion is one of the most important things to be looked after. My advise to any one keeping a public place, is to see to it that the toilet rooms are comfortably heated in winter, to prevent the water pipes from freezing, which is not only very annoying, but also expensive for the necessary repairs. In summer the toilet rooms should be well lighted and ventilated, and have a supply of pure air at all times. These rules should be strictly observed in every barroom. Where ample space can be devoted to the toilet rooms, and it is very important that it should, a washstand, mirror, towel, brush, comb and cuspidores, as well as plenty of toilet paper will add to the comfort of those using them.

15. HOW TO HANDLE LIQUORS IN CASKS OR BOTTLES PROPERLY.

In handling liquors, such as Brandies, Whiskies, Gin, etc., in casks it is well to have them placed on skids, in a place where the temparature is warm, as that will gradually improve the quality of the liquors. Bottled liquors are best placed in a lying position not standing, so that the corks are kept moist at all times, otherwise the strength of the liquor will evaporate. In drawing liquors from a cask, care must be taken to replace the bung; if this is neglected the flavor and strength of the liquor will escape and insects or other things are liable to drop into the liquor.

16. TO KNOW HOW A CUSTOMER DESIRES HIS DRINK TO BE MIXED.

The greatest accomplishment of a bartender lies in exactly suiting his customer. This is done by inquiring what kind of a drink he wishes to have and how he desires to have it mixed; this is especially necessary with cocktails, sours, punches, etc.; the bartender must also inquire, whether the customer desires his drink stiff, strong or medium, and then he must use his own judgment in preparing it, but at all times he must make it a special point to study the tastes of his customers and strictly obey them, and mix all drinks according to their taste. In following this rule, the barkeeper will soon gain the esteem and respect of his patrons.

17. RELATING TO PUNCH BOWLS.

It is of importance to know how to properly cool punches. To do it in the right way, take a metal dish of sufficient size to hold the bowl containing the punch, put the bowl inside of this and completely fill the space between the bowl and the dish with finely shaved ice, on which a little rock salt is sprinkled to prevent it from melting quickly; in letting the ice reach over the rim of the bowl and spreading a few leaves over it, or otherwise ornamenting it, the bartender can produce a nice effect, and will always have a cool and refreshing punch. Decorate the outside of the dish by laying a bright colored napkin or towel around it, then place your punch glasses around the bowl, and the whole arrangement will look pretty and inviting.

18. HOW DRINKS SHOULD BE SERVED AT TABLES.

When the bartender receives an order for drinks to be served at tables, he should send the bottles and ice-water along with the glasses on a tray, so that the parties can help themselves; if there is a check system, the check should be sent along at the same time; if not, it is the bartenders duty to mark down the amount at once to avoid confusion afterwards. Even if there is a check system it is advisable for the barkeeper to put the amount of the check sent on a slate or piece of paper, especially if the bartender does not know the character of the customers.

19. HOW CLARET WINES SHOULD BE HANDLED, ETC.

Claret Wines must be handled with great care; they should be kept in a temperature of 60—70 degrees in a horizontal position, and in serving them, especially in drawing the cork, shaking of the bottle should be avoided, or the sediment, which all clarets deposit, will be mixed with the wine, causing it to look murky. If too cold the bartender may have to place the bottle in warm water or steam the glasses to give the wine the desired temperature, which will always improve its flavor.

20. PURCHASING SUPPLIES.

In purchasing supplies it is advisable and profitable to deal with first-class, reliable firms only, to obtain the best of goods. You will find that it pays best in the long run, to sell a good article at a fair profit. This will give a good reputation and gain the confidence of patrons.

21. HOW TO HANDLE ALE AND PORTER IN CASKS.

In laying in your stock of Ale and Porter, see to it, that you have a sufficiently large stock, as some ales require considerable time to settle and get clear; Bass's Ale for example requires from one to six weeks, before it gets perfectly clear and fit to draw. Stock or Old Ale also requires plenty of time to settle. Ale or Porter should be tapped as soon as placed on the skids, and all shaking of the barrels on tap or to be drawn should be carefully avoided. New Ales require less time to be fit to draw, but it is advisable to have a good stock on hand, as storing will improve the Ale and give better satisfaction to the customer. Keep all Ale and Porter, also those that are bottled in a moderate temperature.

22. HOW ALE AND PORTER SHOULD BE DRAWN.

The proper way.of drawing Ale or Porter is directly from the cask, or as it is called from the wood; if the necessary room and convenience is available the customer prefers this to any other method. If drawn through pipes it is necessary to see to it, that these are made from the best material and constantly kept clean, and that the portion remaining in the pipes over night is not used, so that customers can always obtain a fresh, clear glass of Ale or Porter. Bottled Ales should be stored in a horizontal position, and only what is intended for use during the next three or four days put upright in a cool place, so that the sediment can settle on the bottom of the bottle. In pouring into glasses care should be taken not to shake the bottles. In cold weather it is not necessary to use ice with Ale or Porter drawn behind the bar; but if the weather is warm the temperature may be regulated by putting ice on the pipes. In pouring Ale out of a bottle, the bartender should avoid shaking the bottle while drawing the cork. If pouring out Bass's or Scotch Ale for one customer, a glass should be selected large enough to hold all the bottle contains, otherwise the portion poured out last will not look as clear as it ought to. If two or three glasses are to be filled, the bartender may take them in his left hand and carefully pour in the Ale, by gently tilting the bottle, and it will look perfectly clear and bright and give full satisfaction to the customers.

23. TREATMENT OF MINERAL WATERS.

It is absolutely necessary to keep mineral waters in a cool place, so that they will be cold enough without using ice, when serving them to customers. Syphons of Selters or Vichy should not be placed directly on ice, as there is great danger that they may explode when coming in direct contact with the

PLATE No. 3.

HARRY JOHNSON'S STYLE OF STRAINING MIXED DRINKS
TO A PARTY OF SIX.
Copyrighted, 1888.

ice. These waters all contain more or less gas and acid, which should not be subjected to sudden changes of temperature; they should be placed in an ice box and allowed to cool off gradually. The proper temperature for these mineral waters would be from 35 to 50 degrees.

24. DECORATING DRINKS WITH FRUIT.

It is customary to ornament mixed drinks with different kinds of fruit; when drinks are strained after being mixed, the fruit is placed in the glass into which the drink is strained; but when straining is not necessary the fruit is placed on top of the drink. The fruit should be handled with a handsome fork, and not with the fingers, but in case of a rush the bartender must do the best he can.

25. IN REFERENCE TO LUNCH.

As it is now customary to serve more or less lunch to patrons, it is of the utmost importance, to see to it, that everything you furnish is properly served, clean and fit to eat; also that the place where the lunch is standing is kept perfectly clean, and no remnants of the lunch strewn on the floor. If this is neglected it will look bad enough to disgust some people.

26. HOW TO HANDLE FRUITS, EGGS AND MILK.

Fruits, eggs and milk must always be kept in a cool and clean place, or in an ice box, to preserve them longer. Fruit cut in slices, left over from the day previous, should not be used, as they will taste stale and spoil a mixed drink. The bartender must be careful to have his milk cans clean, and not pour fresh milk to milk left over, as this will cause the milk to sour; the can should be kept tightly closed. In using eggs for mixed drinks, use a separate glass into which to to put the egg, and make sure that it is fresh before mixing it with the drink, otherwise you are liable to spoil the whole drink.

27. HOW CORKS SHOULD BE DRAWN FROM WINE BOTTLES.

The proper way to draw a cork from a wine bottle is to first cut off the top of the tin-foil cap with a knife, then insert the corkscrew and draw the cork. By doing this, the other part of the cap will remain on the bottle, which will look better. How bottled wine should be served has been previously described.

28. HANDLING OF CHAMPAGNES AND OTHER WINES, ETC.

Champagne baskets or cases should be opened carefully, to avoid breakage. Not more than is needed for immediate use should be placed on ice; but if more has been put on ice than called for, it should be left there and not removed, as it will lose strength and flavor if allowed to get warm, and is then again put on ice. If left on the ice, it should be kept close to the freezing point, and the bottles placed so that the labels are not spoiled by ice or water. The bartender must handle champagne carefully, as the bottles easily break on account of the gas contained in the champagne. Champagnes, as well as other wines, such as Rhine Wines, Moselle, Sherry, Port, Claret, etc., should be laid down in storing.

29. CLEANING SILVERWARE, MIRRORS, ETC.

It will be found a simple matter to clean silverware, by observing the following suggestions: Take No. 2 Whitening, dissolve it well in water or spirits, until it becomes as liquid as water; then, after washing off the silverware, apply your whitening in a thin layer and let it get dry, then rub it off with a towel and polish up with a chamois; if unable to reach all the crevices with the chamois, use the silver brush, until every particle of whitening is removed. In cleaning mirrors, wipe off the glass with a damp and clean towel, until all spots are rubbed off from the glass, then take a perfectly clean towel or chamois and polish until the mirror is clean and bright. Use none but linen towels, the same as used for glassware.

30. CORDIALS, BITTERS AND SYRUPS.

Cordials, Bitters and Syrups should not be placed on ice, but kept in a moderate temperature. Those cordials that are used frequently should be kept in small mixing bottles behind the bar and proper care taken to prevent insects from entering them, and spoil the mixture of the drink. In using these mixing bottles it is advisable to keep one finger on the stopper or squirt to prevent it from dropping into the mixing tumbler which would spoil the drink and waste the material.

31. GLASSWARE FOR STRAINED DRINKS.

Attention must be given, to have your glasses of the right size and style, sufficiently large to hold the mixed drinks you intend to strain into them. Mixed drinks will show to better advantage if served in a handsome style of glassware.

32. HANDING BAR-SPOONS TO CUS-TOMERS.

In serving mixed drinks it is proper to give a short-handled bar-spoon with them, so that if the customer desires to take out some of the fruit it contains, such as a slice of orange, a strawberry or a slice of pineapple, he can do so without putting his fingers into the glass. Gentlemen often find it inconvenient to remove their gloves while drinking, therefore a bar-spoon should be given with any mixed drink containing fruit.

33. THE ICE BOX.

It is a very important matter to have the ice box in good condition and perfectly clean, and have all supplies, that are generally kept in the ice box so arranged that you can lay your hand on them without making a long search for them. See to it that the waste pipes leading from the ice box are kept clean and in working order, to avoid trouble. For anyone intending to build an ice box it is of the utmost importance to have it large enough and constructed out of the best material, to have the walls lined with sawdust or other non-conducting materials and the edges or sills covered with galvanized iron or any other metal to protect the woodwork. Also have it constructed in such a manner that it can be easily ventilated whenever found necessary.

34. HOW TO KEEP CELLAR AND STORE-ROOM.

Have storeroom and cellar look as clean as possible and have them well ventilated, so that the air in them will be fresh and clear, and devoid of the foul odors found in some of them. They should be kept in as good condition as the barroom itself. Have the bottled goods and other storeroom supplies in good trim and so separated from each other that each class of goods has its own place, and can easily be found at any time, without searching for them. The cellar floor should be kept clean and dry, and must be looked after, when filling the ice house in summer, and put in good order again. Keep your empty bottles separate and place them on a shelf, in order to have them handy when wanted.

35 GETTING YOUR MONEY WHEN BUSY OR IN A RUSH.

To get your money is the most important and leading point of the business, and should be as strictly attended to as everything else. The correct way of doing this is to calculate the amount while preparing the drinks and place your check in a gentlemanly way in front of the party immediately after waiting upon them. In case of a rush, it is the bartenders duty to be smart and quick in order to get the money, and allow nobody to escape without paying. In making your own cash, it is proper to hand the change due to the customer in a neat and genteel manner, and place it on a dry spot of the counter; so that if a mistake occurs it can easily be rectified.

36. HOW TO CLEAN BRASS AND OTHER METALS.

Most people running a public house take pride in having brass and other metals look as bright as they can be made. By taking good care of ale and liquor measures, beer drips and other metal articles, you will find that not half the work is necessary to keep them shining than some people imagine. All you have to do is to attend to them properly every day.

37. HAVING A COMPLETE PRICE LIST.

It is the proper thing for any public house to have a plain and distinct price list. It will be found advantageous and will avoid a great many mistakes, especially in the sale of bottled goods, or, when the bartender is a stranger behind the bar, and not thoroughly posted in regard to prices of bottled goods, making it impossible for him to act justly towards his employer and the party he sells the goods to

38. KEEPING OF GLASSWARE.

The bartenders particular attention must be given to keeping the glassware in a clean and bright condition. The glasses he hands out to customers to help themselves, as well as the glasses he uses for mixing drinks must be clean and bright and not a speck on them. After using them they should be washed perfectly clean, left on the bench for a little while, and then polished up with nothing but a clean linen glass towel.

39. CIGARS SOLD AT THE BAR.

Where it is the bartenders duty to handle the cigars sold in the business, he should see to it that they give satisfaction. As far as the season is concerned, cigars do not require much attention in summer, they will be moist enough to give satisfaction; but in winter when the atmosphere is very dry, it is advisable to place a wet sponge in the cigar case; this will keep the cigars in good condition.

40. TO KEEP ANTS AND OTHER INSECTS OUT OF MIXING BOTTLES.

Some bartenders find it difficult to keep insects out of the mixing bottles, although it is an easy matter if they take a small china or glass dish, pour some water into it and place the bottle containing the syrup, etc., in the centre of it, which will prevent insects from getting into the bottle. Where the bottles are left standing over night, or any length of time without using, put a little plug into the squirt, or take the squirt stopper out and replace it by an ordinary cork, until you use the bottles again.

41. COVERING BAR FIXTURES WITH GAUZE IN SUMMER.

It is customary to cover the bar and gas fixtures in summer with gauze, to keep them from being soiled by flies and other insects. This should be done in a neat and tasteful manner, and before it is done, the woodwork, chandeliers and mirrors thoroughly cleaned.

42. HOW TO HANDLE ICE.

It is proper to weigh the ice you receive or have it weighed on your own scales. See that the ice received is perfectly free from snow and dirt. Wash all ice thoroughly before putting it in the ice box or behind the bar. The ice used for mixed drinks should be perfectly clear, and when broken up should be handled with an ice scoop and not with your fingers.

43. LAST BUT NOT LEAST.

I cannot avoid very well to offer a few more remarks regarding the conduct and appearance of the bartender, although I touched the subject quite frequently in the book. I wish to impress it on the mind of each man behind the bar, that he should look and act as neat as possible. They should not, like some bartenders do, have a toothpick in their mouth, or clean their finger nails, smoke or spit on the floor, or have other disgusting habits. If it can be avoided they should not eat their meals behind the bar. There are other places where these things can be done without being objectionable to others. After leaving the toilet room a bartender should wash his hands. At all times his hands should be clean and as dry as possible. The swaggering air some bartenders have, and by which they think they impress the customers with their importance, should be studiously avoided.

44. COMPLETE LIST OF UTENSILS, ETC., USED IN A BARROOM.

In giving the annexed list of utensils, used in a barroom, the author wishes it understood that not all the articles mentioned are absolutely necessary in every barroom, but they are indispensable in those places where the business demands call for them, for instance in first-class barrooms

Liquor Measures:
Gallon,
Half-Gallon,
Quart,
Pint,
Half-pint,
Gill,
Half-Gill,
Liquor Pump,
Mallet,
Filtering Bag or Paper,
Beer and Ale Faucets,
Brace and Bit,
Liquor Gauge,
Gimlet,
Beer and Ale Measures,
Bung Starter,
Rubber Hose for drawing Liquor,
Liquor thieves,
Thermometer,
Funnels,
Corkscrews,
Hot Water Kettle,
Bar Pitchers,
Lemon Squeezers,
Beer and Ale Vent,
Ice Pick,
Ice Cooler,
Ice Shaver,

Ice Scoop,
Liquor Gigger,
Shaker,
Long twisted and short Bar Spoons,
Julep and Milk Punch Strainers,
Spice Dish or Castor,
Ale Mugs,
Cork Pullers,
Glass & Scrubbing Brush,
Corks & Stoppers, (different sizes,)
Cork Press,
Champagne Faucets, for drawing Wine out of bottles.
Molasses Jugs or Pitchers
Honey or Syrup Pitchers,
Lemon Knives,
Sugar Spoons,
Sugar Tongues,
Egg Beaters,
Sugar Pails,
Nutmeg Box,
Nutmeg Grater,
Cracker Bowls,
Sugar Bowls,
Punch or Tom and Jerry Bowls, ·

PLATE No. 4.

CHAMPAGNE COCKTAIL.

Tom and Jerry Cups,
Pepper Boxes,
Fruit Dishes,
Punch Ladles,
Duster and Broom,
Silver Brush,
Segar Cutter,
Mop Handle and Wringer
Glass Towels,
Rollers,
Bar Towels,
Spittoons,
Fancy Fruit Forks,
Fancy Sugar Plate or
  Basket,
Liquor Labels,
Pails for Waste,
Match Boxes & Matches,
Comb and Brush,
Toilet Paper,
Whiting for cleaning Sil-
  verware,
Wrapping Paper for Bot-
  tled Goods,
Toothpicks,
Twine,
Writing Paper,
Envelopes,
Postal Cards,
Stamps,
Ink,
Mucilage,
Rattan,

Business Cards,
Business Directory,
City Directory,
Newspapers,
Set of Books,
Wash Soap,
Washing Soda,
Demijohns, (large and
  small),
Bar Bottles,
Mixture Bottles,
Quart Flasks,
Pint Flasks,
Half-pint Flasks,
Segar Bags,
Julep Straws,
Sponge,
Window Brush,
Dust Pan,
Shot for cleaning Bottles,
Step-ladder,
Waiters or Trays,
Oil for oiling the fixtures,
Table Salt and Selery
  Salt Boxes,
Rail Road Guide, (con-
  taining the time table
  for information of diff-
  erent roads,)
Ruler, (for skimming off
  Beerfroth,)
Hammer,
Screws and Nails.

45. LIST OF GLASSWARE,
required in a barroom like the one illustrated:

Goblets for Champagne,
And special glasses for
  the following drinks:

Champagne Cocktail,
Champagne Wine,
John and Tom Collins, ·

3

Julep or Cobbler,
Claret Wine,
Rhine Wine,
Port Wine,
Sherry Wine,
Mineral Water,
Hot Water,
Absinthe and Strainer,
Cocktail and Sour,
Whiskey,
Pony Brandy,

Cordial,
Water,
Hot Apple-toddy,
Ale, Porter and Beer,
Pony Beer,
Ale Mugs,
Tom and Jerry Cups,
Finger Bowls, (for plac-
ing your Bar-spoons
and Strainers,
Glass Jar for Julep Straws

In buying Glassware, match them as near as possible, and have them all the same style.

46. LIST OF LIQUORS
that are required in a barroom:

Brandy, (different brands
if required,)
Bourbon Whiskey,
Scotch Whiskey,
Old Tom Gin,
St. Croix Rum,
Blackberry-Brandy,
Spirits,

Rye Whiskey,
Irish Whiskey,
Holland Gin,
Jamaica Rum,
Apple Jack or Brandy,
Arrack,
Medford Rum,

47. LIST OF WINES.

Champagne,
Sauterne Wines,
Rhine and Moselle Wines,
Bordeaux Wines,
Catawba Wines,
Spanish Wines,
Port, (red and white)
Wines,

Claret Wines,
Madeira Wines,
Hungarian, (red & white)
Wines,
California Wines,
Tokay Wines,
Sherry Wines,
Burgundy Wines,

48. LIST OF CORDIALS.

The list below contains the principal kinds used for mixing drinks, if others are required they can be procured.

Absinthe, (green & white)
Curaçoa (red & white),
Maraschino dalmatico,
Creme de Mocca,
Anisette de Martinique,
Eau D'amour, (Liebes-Wasser),
Vermouth,
Allash Russian Kümmel,
Creme de Mocca,
Vanille,
Creme d'Ananas,
China-China,
Creme d'Anisette,
Huile de fleurs d'oranges,
Creme de Peppermint,
Amourette,
Eau de Calame, (calmus liqueur),
Creme de Nagau,
Creme de Chocolade,
Angelica,
Eau Celeste, (Himmels-Wasser),
Boonekamp of Magbitter,
Creme au lait, (Milk Liqueur),
Benedictine,
Chartreuse, (green and yellow),
Eau d'or A (Goldwasser),
Parfait d'Amour,

Curaçoa de Marseille,
Kirschwasser,
Anisette,
Danziger Goldwasser,
Bouquet de Dames,
Berlin Gilka,
Eau de belles femmes,
Huile d'Angelica,
Eau de pucelle (Jungfern-Wasser),
Maraschino di Zara,
Curaçoa Imperial,
Creme aux Bergamottes,
Creme de Canelle,
Mint Cordial,
Eau d'argent (Silberwasser),
Creme de Cacao,
Krambambuli,
Creme de Meuthe, (Pfefferminz Liqueur),
Creme aux Amandes, (Mandel Creme),
Liqueur de la Grande Chartreuse, (white),
Liqueur de la Grande Chartreuse, (green),
Liqueur de la Grande Chartreuse, (yellow),
Creme de Noisette a la Rose,

49. LIST OF ALES AND PORTER.

Bass Ale in casks and bottles,
Scotch Ales(Muir & Sons),
Scotch Ales (Robert Youn-
kers,)
New and Old Ales,
Bottled Beer, (domestic and imported),

Guinness Extra Stout in casks and bottles, (im-
ported),
Stock Ales,
Porter, Lagerbeer,
Bottled Ales and Porter, (domestic and impor-
ted),

50. LIST OF MINERAL WATERS.

Belfast Ginger Ale,
Kissengen Waters,
Congress Waters,
Vichy Waters,
Lemon and Plain Soda Waters,
Sarsaparilla,
Carbonic Acid, ·

Domestic Ginger Ale,
Apollinaris Waters,
Imp. Selters Waters,
Syphon Selters Waters,
Hathorn Waters,
Cider,
Acid Syphon,

51. LIST OF SYRUPS.

White Gum Syrup,
Pineapple Syrup,
Strawberry Syrup,
Raspberry Syrup,
Lemon Syrup,

Orange Syrup,
Orchard Syrup,
Orgeat Syrup,
Rock Candy Syrup,

52. LIST OF BITTERS.

Boker's (the genuine only) is preferred everywhere at the present time,
Hostetters Bitters,

Orange Bitters,
Boonecamp Bitters,
Stoughton Bitters,
Sherry Wine Bitters,

53. LIST OF FRUITS.

Apples,
Peaches,
Limes,
Grapes,
Blackberries,

Oranges,
Lemons,
Pineapples,
Strawberries,

54. LIST OF MIXTURES.

Tansy,
Calamus or Flag Root,
Black Molasses,
Milk,
Jamaica Ginger,
Mint,
Honey,
Wormwood,
Eggs,
Sugar, (lumps and pulverized,)
Peppermint,
Pepper, (red and black,)
Condensed Milk,

Nutmeg,
Allspice,
Cinnamon,
Salt,
Pepper Sauce,
Bicarbonate of Soda,
Calisaya,
Cloves,
Coffee,
Roast Corn,
Celery Salt,
Beef Extract,
Celery Syrup.

55. SUNDRIES.

Segars,
Cigarettes,

Tobaccos,
Chewing Tobacco.

56. CHAMPAGNE COCKTAILS.
(Use a champagne goblet.)

In mixing all the different cocktails, it is proper to fill the mixing tumbler with fine shaved or broken ice, before putting in any of the ingredients; as it has a much better appearance, but in mixing a Champagne Cocktail it is the proper way of having two or three lumps of clear crystal ice, place them on the bottom of your glass, and mix as follows:

2 or 3 small lumps of crystal ice;

1 or 2 slices of orange, placed on top of the ice;

2 or 3 nice strawberries (if in season);

1 fine slice of pineapple;

1 lump of loaf sugar placed on top ot the ice;

2 or 3 dashes of bitters; (Boker's genuine only.)

In all first-class barrooms Boker's Genuine Bitters is still in demand as much as ever.

Fill the Champagne Cocktail glass with wine, stir up well with a spoon and twist a nice piece of lemon peel on top of this, and serve. If it should happen, as it is often the case, that a party of two or three should enter the barroom, and call for a Champagne Cocktail, the proper way would be for a bartender to inquire what kind of wine they desire; a small bottle being sufficient for three cocktails, and also see that the sugar is handled at all times with a pair of tongues, and the fruit with a fork; this is strictly to be observed in mixing the above drink. (See Illustration, Plate No. 4.)

57 MARTINI COCKTAIL.
(Use a large bar glass.)

Fill the glass up with ice;

2 or 3 dashes of Gum Syrup;

2 or 3 dashes of Bitters; (Boker's genuine only.)

1 dash of Curaçoa;
$^1/_2$ wine glassful of Old Tom Gin;
$^1/_2$ "   "   " Vermouth;
stir up well with a spoon, strain it into a fancy
cocktail glass, squeeze a piece of lemon peel on top,
and serve. (See Ilustration, Plate No. 13.)

58. CHAMPAGNE SOUR.
(Use a fancy glass.)

1 lump of loaf sugar;
2 dashes of fresh lemon juice;
place the saturated sugar into a fancy glass, also
a slice of orange and a slice of pineapple, a few
strawberries or grapes (if in season), fill up the glass
slowly with Champagne, and stir up well, and
serve it. (See Illustration, Plate No. 5.)

59. MORNING GLORY FIZZ.
(Use a large bar glass.)

In all first-class barrooms it is proper to have the
whites of eggs separated into an empty bottle,
provided you have a demand for such a drink,
and keep them continually on ice, and by doing
so, considerable time will be saved; mix as follows:
1 fresh egg (the white only);
$^3/_4$ table-spoonful of sugar;
1 or 2 dashes of lemon juice;
2 or 3 dashes of lime juice;
3 to 4 dashes of absinthe, dissolved well with a
   little water;
$^3/_4$ glass filled with fine shaved ice;
1 wine glass of Scotch whiskey;
shake up well with a shaker; strain it into a good
sized bar glass; fill up the balance with Syphon
Selters or Vichy Water, and serve.
    The above drink must be drank as soon as pre-
pared so as not to lose the effect and flavor. The
author respectfully recommends the above drink

as an excellent one for a morning beverage, which will give a good appetite and quiet the nerves. (See Illustration, Plate No. 7.)

60. CHAMPAGNE JULEP.
(Use a fancy Champagne Julep glass.)

Take the sugar tongues and place 1 lump of loaf sugar into the glass, add 1 long sprig of fresh mint, then pour your champagne into the glass very slowly, and while doing so, keep on stirring gently all the time; place a piece of orange and a few strawberries (if in season) on top, and serve.

The above drink does not require to be stirred up as much as other Juleps, or else the Champagne will lose its flavor and natural taste, and foam to much. (See Illustration, Plate No. 14.)

61. MANHATTAN COCKTAIL.
(Use a large bar glass.)

Fill the glass up with ice;
2 or 3 dashes of Gum Syrup;
1 or 2 dashes of Bitters; (Boker's genuine only);
1 dash of Curaçoa (or absinthe if required);
$1/2$ wine glass of Whiskey·
$1/2$ wine glass of Vermouth;
stir up well, strain into a fancy cocktail glass, squeeze a piece of lemon peel on the top, and serve; leave it for the customer to decide whether to use Absinthe or not. This drink is very popular at the present day.

62. CURACOA PUNCH.
(Use a large bar glass.)

$1/2$ table spoonful of sugar;
2 or 3 dashes of lemon juice;
$1/2$ wine glass of water, dissolve well with a
 spoon; Fill up the glass with fine shaved ice;
$1/2$ wine glass of brandy;
1 " " " curaçoa; (red)

$^1/_2$ pony glass of Jamaica rum; stir up well with a spoon, ornament with grapes, pineapple, orange and berries (if in season) and serve with a straw

The above drink if mixed correctly, is very delicious. (See Illustration, Plate No. 12.)

63. MINT JULEP.
(Use a large bar glass.)

1 table-spoonful of sugar;
$^1/_2$ Wine glass of water or Selters;
3 or 4 sprigs of fresh mint; dissolve with sugar
and water, until the flavor of the mint is well
extracted, then take out the mint; add
1$^1/_2$ wine glass of Brandy;
Fill the glass with fine shaved ice; stir well, then take some sprigs of mint and insert them in the ice with the stem downward, so that, the leaves will be above in the shape of a bouquet; ornament with berries, pineapple and orange on top in a tasty manner; dash with a little Jamaica rum, and sprinkle with a little sugar on top; serve with a straw.

This drink is known not only in this country, but in all parts of the world, by name and reputation. (See Illustration, Plate No. 8.)

64. POUSSE CAFÉ.
(Use a Sherry wine glass.)

In mixing the above drink, which is a favorite drink of the French, and also has become a favorite in this country, great care must be taken. As there are several liquors required in the preparation of this drink, it should be made in a manner that the portions will be perfectly separated from each other, therefore, I would suggest, that a sherry wine glass would be used for pouring in these different Cordials, instead of a tea-spoon, or the original bottles, as it has a better appearance and takes less time; mix as follows;

$^1/_6$ glass of Parfait d'Amour or Raspberry syrup;
$^1/_6$ glass of Maraschino;
$^1/_6$ glass of Vanilla, (green);
$^1/_6$ glass of Curaçoa, (red);
$^1/_6$ glass of Chartreuse, (yellow);
$^1/_6$ glass of Cognac (or Brandy;)

The above ingredients will fill the glass. (See Illustration, Plate No. 6.)

I would advise any bartender having calls for these drinks often, to place his original bottles containing the different Cordials used in the drink separate in one place, so as to have them follow in the rotation above mentioned; this will avoid mixing up the bottles and trouble. I also have to mention another item of great importance, and that is, that the Cordials used in the above drink differ in weight, for instance, you will find the French Curaçoa to weigh more than the Holland Curaçoa, and so it is different in all Cordials and it is wise for a bartender to find out the different weights and then place them in rotation, in order to avoid mixing up; therefore you cannot depend entirely on the illustration in mixing the drink called Pousse Café.

65. POUSSE L'AMOUR.
(Use a Sherry wine glass.)

This delicious French drink is somewhat similar to the Pousse Café, and also has to be carefully made; mix as follows;

$^1/_4$ sherry glass of Maraschino, drop in
1 yolk of a fresh Egg;
$^1/_4$ glass of Vanilla, (green);
$^1/_4$ glass of Cognac;

Proper attention must be paid that the yolk of the egg does not run into the liquor, in order to have it in its natural form. (See Illustration, Plate No. 6.)

66. BRANDY CRUSTA.
(Use a large bar glass.)

Take a nice, clean lemon of the same size as your
wine glass, cut off both ends of it, and peel it the
same as you would an apple, put the lemon peel
in the wine glass, so that it will line the entire
inside of the glass, and dip the edge of the glass
and lemon peel in pulverized sugar, take your
mixing glass and mix as follows:
3 or 4 dashes of Orchard syrup;
1 or 2 dashes of Bitters (Boker's genuine only);
4 or 5 drops of Lemon juice;
2 dashes of Maraschino;
$3/4$ of the glass filled with fine ice;
1 wine glass of Brandy;
stir up well with a spoon, strain it into the glass,
dress with a little fruit, and serve. (See Illustration,
Plate No. 5.)

67. FANCY WHISKEY SMASH.
(Use a large bar glass.)

$1/2$ table-spoonful of Sugar;
$1/2$ glass of Water, or squirt of Selters;
3 or 4 sprigs of mint, dissolve well with a spoon;
Fill the glass full of fine shaved ice;
1 wine glass of Whiskey;
stir up well with a spoon; strain it into a fancy
sour glass, ornament with fruit, and serve.
This drink requires particular care and attention,
so as to have it palatable and look proper.

68. WHISKEY DAISY.
(Use a large bar glass.)

$1/2$ table-spoonful of sugar;
2 or 3 dashes of Lemon juice;
1 dash of Lime juice;
1 squirt of Syphon Selters, dissolve with the
lemon and lime juice;

³/₄ of the glass filled with fine shaved ice;
1 wine glass of good Whiskey;
Fill the glass with shaved ice;
½ pony glass Chartreuse (yellow);
stir up well with a spoon, then take a fancy glass
have it dressed with fruit and strain the mixture
into it, and serve.

This drink is very palatable and will taste good
to most anybody. (See Illustration, Plate No. 10.)

69. CHAMPAGNE COBBLER.
(Use a large bar glass.)

¼ of a table-spoonful of sugar;
¼ wine glass of Syphon Selters, dissolve well;
1 or 2 pieces of Orange;
1 or 2 pieces of Pineapple;
Fill the glass with ice;
Fill the balance with champagne, ornament the top
in a tasty manner, and serve it with a straw.

This drink is generally mixed where they have
champagne on draught, by having the champagne
faucet screwed into the cork of the bottle. (See
Illustration, Plate No. 8.)

70. ROMAN PUNCH.
(Use a large bar glass.)

½ table-spoonful of sugar;
½ pony glass of Raspberry syrup;
2 or 3 dashes of Lemon juice, dissolve with a
        little water or Selters;
¼ pony glass of Curaçoa;
½ wine glass of Brandy;
½ pony glass of Jamaica rum;
stir up well with a spoon, ornament the top with
grapes, oranges, pineapple, etc., (if in season,) and
serve with a straw.

This is one of the oldest drinks known. (See
Illustration, Plate, No. 14.)

71. GOLDEN SLIPPER.
(Use a Sherry wine glass.)

$^1/_2$ wine glass of Chartreuse (yellow);
1 yolk of a fresh cold egg;
$^1/_2$ wine glass of Danziger Goldwasser;
The above drink is a great favorite of the ladies
from Southern America, and must be mixed in a
very careful manner, so that the yolk of the egg
does not run into the liquor, and keep its form.
(See Illustration, Plate No. 13.)

72. MISSISSIPPI PUNCH.
(Use a large bar glass.)

1 table-spoonful of sugar;
$^1/_2$ wine glass of Water or Selters;
2 dashes of lemon juice, dissolved well;
$^1/_2$ wine glass of Jamaica rum;
$^1/_2$ wine glass of Bourbon whiskey;
1 wine glass of Brandy;
fill the glass with shaved ice; shake or stir the
ingredients well, ornament in a tasty manner with
fruit in season, and serve with a straw. (See Illustration, Plate No. 12.)

73. SILVER FIZZ.
(Use a large bar glass.)

$^1/_2$ table-spoonful of sugar;
2 or 3 dashes of Lemon juice;
1 wine glass of Old Tom Gin, dissolved well, with
    a squirt of Vichy;
1 egg, (the white only);
$^3/_4$ glass filled with shaved ice;
shake up well with a shaker, strain it into a good
sized fizz glass, fill up the glass with Syphon Selters
or Vichy water, mix well and serve.
    This drink is a delicious one, and must be drank
as soon as prepared, as it loses its strength and
flavor.

74. BRANDY CHAMPARELLE.
(Use a Sherry wine glass.)

$^1/_4$ wine glass of Curaçoa (red);
$^1/_4$ wine glass of Chartreuse (yellow);
$^1/_4$ wine glass of Anisette;
$^1/_4$ wine glass of Kirschwasser or Brandy;
whichever the customer desires, and serve.

Attention must be paid to prevent the different liquors from running into each other, to have them perfectly separated and distinct.
(See illustration, Plate No. 6.)

75. VANILLA PUNCH.
(Use a large bar glass.)

1 table-spoonful of sugar;
2 or 3 dashes of lime or lemon juice;
2 or 3 dashes of Curaçoa dissolve well with a little water or selters. Fill up the glass with shaved ice.
1 pony glass of brandy;
$1^1/_2$ wine glass of Vanilla; mixed well with a spoon; ornament with Fruit in a tasty manner, and serve with a straw.

76. KNICKERBOCKER.
(Use a large bar glass.)

2 table-spoonfuls of Raspberry syrup;
2 dashes of Lemon juice;
1 slice of Pineapple;
1 slice of Orange;
1 wine glass full of St. Croix rum;
$^1/_2$ wine glass of Curaçoa;
then fill the glass with fine shaved ice, stir or shake well, and dress with Fruit in season; serve with a straw.

77. TOLEDO PUNCH.
(Use a large punch bowl.)

This punch is only prepared for parties, and the author composed it for one of the most prominent establishments in the West, and styled it "Toledo."
Mix as follows:
Place 2 pounds of loaf sugar in the bowl;
4 or 5 bottles of plain soda water;
4 Lemons, the juice only;
1 qt. of French Cognac;
1 small bunch of Wintergreen;
4 Oranges and 1 Pineapple (cut up);
and add the slices into the bowl and also Strawberries and Grapes in season;
Mix the ingredients well with a spoon or ladle and add:
6 bottles of Champagne;
1 bottle of Brandy;
2 bottles of French Claret;
4 bottles of Rhine Wine;
1¹/₂ gallon of Water and mix up well together into the bowl, and you will have one of the finest punches ever made.
It is understood that this punch must be cold, surrounded with ice, the same as other punches.
After having the entire punch well mixed, take a large fancy goblet, and fill it with the above mixture and dress it with oranges, strawberries, pineapples in season, etc., etc.

78. ABSINTHE COCKTAIL.
(Use a large bar glass.)

Fill up with ice;
3 or 4 dashes of gum syrup;
1 dash of Bitters (Boker's genuine only);
1 dash of Anisette;
¹/₄ wine glass of water;
³/₄ wine glass of Absinthe;

shake well until almost frozen, strain it into a fancy cocktail glass; squeeze a lemon peel on top, and serve.

This drink is liked by the French and by Americans, it is an elegant beverage and a splendid appetizer, but see that you always have only the genuine Absinth for mixing this drink.

79. SHERRY COBBLER.
(Use a large bar glass.)

$^1/_2$ table-spoonful of sugar;
$^1/_2$ wine glass of water, dissolve with a spoon;
fill the glass up with fine crystal ice;
then fill the glass up with Sherry wine;
stir well with a spoon, and ornament with grapes, oranges, pineapples, berries, etc., serve with a straw.

This drink is without doubt the most popular beverage in the country, with ladies as well as with gentlemen. It is a very refreshing drink for old and young.

80. SHERRY FLIP.
(Use a large bar glass.)

1 Fresh Egg;
$^1/_2$ table-spoonful of sugar;
$^1/_2$ glassful of shaved ice;
$1^1/_2$ wine glass full of Sherry wine;
shake it well, until it is thoroughly mixed, strain it into a fancy bar glass, grate a little nutmeg on top and serve.

This is a very delicious drink and gives strength to delicate people. (See illustration, Plate No. 15.)

81. BRANDY PUNCH.
(Use a large bar glass.)

$^3/_4$ table-spoonful of sugar;
A few drops of Pineapple syrup;
1 or 2 dashes of Lemon juice;
1 or 2 dashes of Lime juice;

CHAMPAGNE SOUR. BRANDY CRUSTA.

1 squirt of Selters; dissolve with a spoon:
Fill up the glass with finely shaved ice;
1¹|₂ wine glassfuls of Old Brandy;
stir up well; flavor with a few drops of Jamaica rum
and ornament with grapes, oranges, pineapple and
berries, and serve with a straw.

82. ST. CHARLES PUNCH.
(Use a large bar glass.)

1 table-spoonful of sugar;
2 or 3 dashes of Lemon juice, dissolve with a little
 water or Selters;
1 wine glass full of Port wine;
1 pony glass of Brandy;
¹/₂ glass of Curaçoa;
Fill the glass with fine ice, stir well with a spoon,
ornament the-top with grapes, oranges, etc., in season
and serve with a straw.
This is one of the most popular summer drinks
known in the South.

83. EGG NOGG.
(Use a large bar glass.)

1 fresh Egg;
³/₄ table-spoonful of sugar;
¹/₃ glass full of ice;
1 pony glass St. Croix or Jamaica rum;
1 wine glass full of Brandy;
Fill the glass with rich milk, shake the ingredients
well together and strain into a large bar glass; grate
a little nutmeg on top and serve. It is proper for
the bartender to ask the customer what flavor he
prefers, whether St. Croix or Jamaica rum.

84. WHITE LION.
(Use a large bar glass.)

1 table-spoonful of sugar;
2 or 3 dashes of Lime or Lemon juice, dissolve well
 with a little water;

4

$^1/_2$ pony glass of Raspberry syrup;
$^1/_4$ pony glass of Curaçoa;
Fill up the glass with shaved ice;
1 wine glass full of St. Croix rum;
stir up well with a spoon; ornament with the fruits-
of the season; serve with a straw.

This drink is known for a great number of years
in South America.

85. BALTIMORE EGG NOGG.
(Use a large bar glass.)

1 yolk of an egg;
$^3/_4$ table-spoonful of sugar;
Add a little nutmeg and cinnamon, and beat to a
    cream;
$^1/_2$ pony glass of Brandy;
3 or 4 lumps of ice;
$^1/_4$ pony glass of Jamaica rum;
1 wine glass full of Madeira wine;
Fill the glass with milk, shake well, strain into a
large bar glass, grate a little nutmeg on top and
serve.

86. FANCY BRANDY COCKTAIL.
(Use a large bar glass.)

$^3/_4$ glass filled with shaved ice;
2 or 3 dashes of Gum syrup;
1 or 2 dashes of Bitters, (Boker's genuine only);
1 or 2 dashes of Curaçoa, or Absinthe if required;
1 glass of French Brandy;
stir well with a spoon, strain into a fancy cocktail
glass and squirt a little champagne into it, twist a
piece of lemon peel on top and serve. The champagne will only be added where it is kept on draught.

Mixed as directed the above will make a very
pleasant drink. It is a universal favorite in the
western part of this country.

87. WHISKEY CRUSTA.

(Use a large bar glass.)

Take a nice clean lemon, the same size as your wine glass, cut off both ends and peel it the same as you would an apple, put the lemon peel in the wine glass so that it will line the entire inside of the glass, then dip the edge of the glass and lemon peel in pulverized sugar. The mixture is as follows;

$^1/_2$ pony glass of Orchard, syrup;
1 or 2 dashes of Bitters (Boker s genuine only);
1 dash of Lemon juice;
2 dashes of Maraschino;
$^1/_2$ glass of fine shaved ice;
$^3/_4$ wine glass of Whiskey;

mix well with a spoon, strain it into the wine glass containing the lemon peel. ornament it with a little fruit, and serve.

88. FANCY BRANDY SMASH.

(Use a large bar glass.)

$^1/_2$ table-spoonful of sugar ;
$^1/_2$ wine glass of Water or Selters;
3 or 4 sprigs of fresh mint, dissolved well;
$^1/_2$ glass of shaved ice;
1 wine glass of Brandy;

stir up well with a spoon, strain it into a fancy bar glass, and ornament it with a little fruit in season, and serve. (See Illustration, Plate No. 9.)

89. SHERRY WINE PUNCH.

(Use a large bar glass.)

$^1/_2$ wine glass of Orchard syrup;
1 dash of Lemon juice;
Fill the glass with fine shaved ice;
$1^1/_2$ wine glass of Sherry wine;

stir up well with a spoon; ornament with grapes, oranges, pineapple and berries; top it off with a little Claret wine, and serve with a straw.

This is a very delicious summer drink and is well-known.

90. BRANDY FIX.
(Use a large bar glass.)

$^1/_2$ table-spoonful of sugar;
2 or 3 dashes of Lime or Lemon juice;
$^1/_2$ pony glass of Pineapple syrup;
1 or 2 dashes of Chartreuse (green), dissolved
  well with a little Water or Selters;
Fill up the glass with shaved ice;
1 wine glass of Brandy;
stir up with a spoon, and ornament the top with
grapes, and berries in season, and serve with a
straw.

91. CLARET PUNCH.
(Use a large bar glass.)

$^3/_4$ table-spoonful of sugar;
. 1 squirt of Selters;
Fill with ice;
$^1/_2$ dash of lemon juice, provided the Claret wine
  if not too sour;
Fill the glass with Claret wine, stir up well with a
  spoon; ornament with oranges, berries, pineapple, etc., in season and serve.
This is a very popular summer drink, and is very
cooling in hot weather.

92. KNICKERBEIN.
(Use a Sherry wine glass.)

$^1/_3$ Sherry wine glass vanilla;
1 fresh egg (the yolk only); cover the egg with
  Benedictine;
$^1/_3$ Sherry wine glass of Kirschwasser or Cognac;
4 to 6 drops of Bitters; (Boker's genuine only.)
Particular care must be taken with the above
drink, the same as with Pousse Café, to prevent the
liquors from running into each other, so that the
yolk of the egg, and the different liquors are kept
separated from each other.

93. SANTINAS POUSSE CAFE.
(Use a Sherry wine glass.

$1/3$ wine glass of Maraschino ;
$1/3$ wine glass of Curaçoa (red);
$1/3$ wine glass of French Brandy ; and serve.
This drink is generally indulged in after partaking of a cup of black coffee, and care must be taken to prevent the different liquors from running into each other, as the proper appearance has a great deal to do with it.

94. SAUTERNE COBBLER
(Use a large bar glass.)

$1/2$ table-spoonful of sugar ;
$1/2$ wine glass Orchard syrup ;
$1/4$ wine glass of water or Selters ; dissolved well
with a spoon ;
Fill the glass with fine shaved ice ;
$1^1/2$ wine glass of Sauterne wine ; stir up well, ornament with grapes, oranges, pineapple. berries, etc., and serve with a straw.

95. MILK PUNCH.
(Use a large bar glass.)

$^*/_4$ table-spoonful sugar ;
$1/3$ glass of fine ice ;
1 wine glass of Brandy ;
$1/2$ wine glass of St. Croix rum ;
Fill the glass with rich milk, shake the ingredients together, strain into a fancy bar glass, grate a little nutmeg on top and serve.

Bartenders must understand that these prescriptions for mixed drinks are strictly and exclusively first-class ; therefore if a bartender works in a place which is not first-class, and is not getting a high price for his drinks, he must use his own judgement about the ingredients, in order not to sell his drinks without profit. For instance where I say Brandy in this mixed drink, Whiskey would have to be taken in place of it, and where the prescription calls for St. Croix rum, take Medford rum, etc. These would be the proper ingredients where a low price is charged for a Milk Punch. This illustration will answer for all other drinks.

96. FAIVRE'S POUSSE CAFE.
(Use a Sherry wine glass.)

$^1/_3$ glassful of Benedictine ;
$^1/_3$ glassful of Curaçoa (red);
$^1/_3$ glassful of Kirschwasser or Brandy ;
2 or 3 drops of Bitters (Boker's genuine only);

Attention must be paid to prevent the different colors from running into each other; they should be kept separate.

97. HOW TO MIX ABSINTHE.
(Use an Absinthe glass.)

In preparing the above drink you must be particular and inquire whether the customer desires it in the old French style or on the new improved plan. Mix as follows in a large bar or Absinthe glass : 1 pony glass of Absinthe, place this into the large glass, take the top part of the Absinthe glass, which has the shape of a bowl, with a small round hole in the bottom, fill this with fine shaved ice, and water ; then raise the bowl up high, and let the water run or drip into the glass containing the Absinthe ; the color of the Absinthe will show when to stop ; then pour into the large glass and serve. None but genuine Absinthe should be used, which you can easily tell by the color in mixing, as it will turn to a milk color and look cloudy, which the domestic article does not. This is what they call an old style French Absinthe.

98. AMERICAN STYLE OF MIXING ABSINTHE.

(Use a large bar glass.)

$^3/_4$ glassful of fine ice;
6 or 7 dashes of gum syrup;
1 pony glass of Absinthe;
2 wine glasses water;
Then shake the ingredients, until the outside of
the shaker is covered with ice; then strain it into
a large bar glass and serve. As this is mixed it is
more pleasant to drink than the French style. The
Americans are not in the habit of drinking Absinthe
like the French, but a drink of it occasionally will
hurt nobody.

This is what they call the American or frozen
Absinthe

99. ITALIAN STYLE OF MIXING ABSINTHE.

(Use a large bar glass.)

1 pony glass of Absinthe;
2 or 3 lumps of broken ice;
2 or 3 dashes of Maraschino;
$^1/_2$ pony glass of Anisette;
Take a small pitcher of ice water, and pour the
water slowly into a large bar glass containing the
mixture, stir with a spoon and serve. This is a very
pleasant way of drinking Absinthe. As it promotes
appetite, it is especially recommended before meals.

100. GERMAN OR SWISS STYLE OF MIX- ING ABSINTHE.

(Use a large bar glass.)

The Germans and Swiss have the simplest way of
drinking Absinthe that I met with in my travels
through Europe. If a person goes to a Café or barroom as we call it, and asks for Absinthe, the bartender or waiter puts a pony glass of Absinthe into a
large tumbler and sends this and a pitcher of water

to the customer, who helps himself to as much water
as he desires, and there is no mixing or fixing up
about it. I consider this a very simple style of
drinking Absinthe, but it tastes just as good to them
and answers the purpose.

101. GOLDEN FIZZ.
(Use a large bar glass.

³/₄ table-spoonful of sugar ;
2 or 3 dashes of lemon juice ;
1 wine glass of Whiskey or Tom Gin (if the cus-
    tomer desires Tom Gin.)
1 Egg (the yolk only) ;
³/₄ glassful of fine shaved ice ;
Shake up well in a shaker, strain it into a good-
sized fizz glass, fill up the glass with Syphon Vichy,
or Selters waters ; mix well with a spoon and serve.
    This drink will suit Old Harry and is very delicious
in the hot season. It must be drank as soon
as mixed, or it will lose its flavor.

102. VERMOUTH COCKTAIL.
(Use a large bar glass.)

³/₄ glass of shaved ice ;
4 or 5 dashes of gum ;
2 or 3 dashes of Bitters (Boker's genuine only) ;
1 wine glass Vermouth ;
2 dashes of Maraschino ;
Stir up well with a spoon; strain it into a cocktail
glass, twist a piece of lemon peel on top, and serve.

103. SELTERS LEMONADE.
(Use a large bar glass.)

1¹/₂ table-spoonfuls of sugar ;
4 to 6 dashes of Lemon juice ;
4 or 5 small lumps of broken ice ;
then fill up the glass with Syphon Selters, stir up
well with a spoon and serve.

If customers desire to have the imported Selters waters, use that instead of the Syphon Selters.

In order to have the above drink mixed properly, you must not spare sugar or lemon juice.

104. PORT WINE PUNCH.
(Use a large bar glass.)

1 glass full of fine ice;
$^1/_2$ table-spoonful of sugar;
$^1/_2$ table-spoonful of Orchard syrup;
1 or 2 dashes of Lemon juice;
$^1/_2$ wine glass full of water, dissolve well with sugar and lemon;
Fill up the glass with Port wine;
mix well with a spoon and ornament the top with grapes, oranges, pineapple and berries, and serve with a straw.

105. WHISKEY JULEP.
(Use a large bar glass.)

$^3/_4$ table-spoonful of sugar;
$^1/_2$ wine glass full of Water or Selters;
3 or 4 sprigs of fresh mint, dissolve well until all the essence of the mint is extracted;
Fill up the glass with fine shaved ice;
1 wine glass full of Whiskey;
stir up well with a spoon and ornament this drink with mint, oranges, pineapples and berries in a tasty manner; sprinkle a little sugar on top of it; dash with Jamaica rum, and serve.

106. BRANDY FLIP.
(Use a large bar glass.)

1 fresh egg;
$^3/_4$ table-spoonful of sugar;
$^3/_4$ glass of shaved ice;
1 wine glass full of Brandy;
shake the above ingredients well in a shaker, strain into a flip or other fancy bar glass, and grate a little nutmeg on top, and serve.

107. ST. CROIX RUM PUNCH.
(Use a large bar glass.)

1 table-spoonful of sugar;
3 or 4 dashes of Lime or Lemon juice;
$\frac{1}{2}$ wine glass of water, dissolve well:
$\frac{1}{4}$ pony glass of Jamaica rum;
1 wine glass of St. Croix rum;
Fill up with fine shaved ice;
mix well with a spoon, ornament with fruit in season, and serve with a straw.

This is a very cooling and pleasant drink in the hot season, providing you don't use poor rum.

108. GENERAL HARRISON EGG NOGG.
(Use a large bar glass.)

. 1 fresh egg;
$\frac{1}{4}$ table-spoonful of sugar;
3 or 4 small lumps of ice;
Fill the glass with Cider;
shake well; strain it into a large bar glass; grate a little nutmeg on top and serve. · ·

The above drink is a very•pleasant one, and is popular throughout the southern part of the country and it is not intoxicating. It is proper to use the very best quality of Cider, as by using poor Cider it is impossible to make this drink palatable.

109. TIP-TOP PUNCH.
(Use a large bar glass.)

3 or 4 lumps of broken ice;
1 pony glass of Brandy;
1 piece of loaf sugar;
1 or 2 slices of orange;
1 or 2 slices of pineapple;
2 or 3 drops of Lemon juice;
Fill up the balance with Champagne;·
mix well with a spoon, dress up the top- with fruits in season, and serve with a straw.

This drink is only mixed where they have Champagne on draught, as mentioned in other receipts.

110. MEDFORD RUM SOUR.

(Use a large bar glass.)

$1/2$ table-spoonful of sugar;
3 or 4 dashes of Lemon juice;
1 squirt of Syphon Selters, dissolved well;
1 wine glass of Medford rum;
Fill $3/4$ of the glass with ice;
stir well with a spoon; strain into a sour glass,
ornament with fruit, etc., and serve.

This is an old Boston drink, and has the reputation of being cooling and pleasant.

111. THE OLD DELAWARE FISHING PUNCH.

(Use a large bar glass.)

1 table-spoonful of sugar;
1 or 2 dashes of Lemon juice;
1 or 2 dashes of Lime juice, dissolve well in a
    little water;
Fill up the glass with fine ice;
1 wine glass of St. Croix rum;
1 pony glass of Old Brandy;
stir up well with a spoon, dress the top with fruit
in season, and serve with a straw.

This drink can also be put up in bottles for the
Fisherman to take along, so that he will loose no
time while fishing.

112. TOM COLLINS.

(Use an extra large bar glass.)

$3/4$ table-spoonful of Sugar;
3 or 4 dashes of Lime or Lemon juice;
3 or 4 pieces of broken ice;
1 wine glass of Old Tom Gin; (genuine only)
1 bottle of plain Soda Water;
mix well with a spoon, remove the ice, and serve.

Attention must be paid not to let the foam of the
soda water spread over the glass; this drink must be
drank as soon as mixed in order not to let it get stale.

113. APPLE JACK SOUR.

(Use a large bar glass.)

$^1/_2$ table-spoonful of Sugar;
2 or 3 dashes of Lemon juice;
1 squirt of Syphon Selters water, dissolve well;
$^3/_4$ glass of fine shaved ice;
1 wine glass of old Cider Brandy or what they call Apple Jack;
stir up with a spoon, strain it into a sour glass, and ornament it with a little fruit, and serve.

This has allways been a very fashionable drink with Jersey people.

114. GIN FIZZ.

(Use a large bar glass.)

$^1/_2$ table-spoonful Sugar;
3 or 4 dashes of Lemon juice;
$^1/_2$ glass of shaved ice;
1 wine glass of Old Tom Gin;
stir up well with a spoon, strain it into a large sized bar glass, fill up the balance with Vichy or Selters water, mix well and serve.

Bear in mind that all drinks called Fizz's, must be drank as soon as handed out, or the natural taste of the same is lost to the customer.

115. ALE SANGAREE.

(Use a large bar glass.)

1 tea-spoonful of Sugar;
$^1/_2$ wine glass of water, dissolve with a spoon;
Fill up the balance with Ale, grate a little nutmeg on top, and serve.

It is customary to ask the customer if he desires Old, New or Mixed Ale; if he desires New Ale, you must prevent the foam from running over the glass; attention must also be paid to the temperature of the Ale, so as to have it not too cold or too warm.

116. BLUE BLAZER.

(Use a large mug with a handle to it.)

$^1/_2$ pony glass of Honey or Rock Candy;
$^1/_2$ wine glass Syrup;
1 wine glass of Whiskey; (Scotch)
mix well with a little hot water, and put it over the
fire and have it boiled up; set the liquid on fire, and
take it quick and pour it from one mug to the other,
pour it so about three or four times in long streams,
until it is well mixed; grate a little nutmeg on top;
this will have the appearance of a continual stream
of fire. Attention must be paid to prevent the fire
from spreading over your hands; pour it into a large
sized bar glass, put a slice of lemon into it, and serve.

This is a very elegant drink in cold weather and
has a wonderful effect of healing an old cold.
Especially when the party goes to bed soon after
drinking it.

117 BOWL OF EGG NOGG FOR A NEW-YEAR'S PARTY.

In regard to this drink the bartender must use
his own judgment and use the proportions in accordance to the quantity to be made. For a three gallon
bowl mix as follows:

$2^1/_2$ lbs. of fine pulverized sugar;
20 fresh eggs; have the yolks separated; beat as
    thin as water, and add the yolks of the eggs
    into the sugar, and dissolve by stirring;
2 quarts of good old Brandy;
$1^1/_2$ pints of Jamaica rum;
2 gallons of good rich milk;
mix the ingredients well with a ladle, and stir continually while pouring in the milk to prevent it from
curdling; then beat the whites of the eggs to a stiff
froth and put this on top of the mixture; then
fill a bar glass with a ladle, put some of the egg

froth on top, grate a little nutmeg over it and serve.
This will give you a splendid Egg Nogg for all New
Years callers.

118. JOHN COLLINS.
(Use an extra large bar glass.)

$^3/_4$ table-spoonful of sugar;
2 or 3 dashes of Lemon juice;
2 dashes of Lime juice;
4 or 5 small lumps of ice;
1 wine glass full of Holland gin;
pour in a bottle of plain soda, mix up well, remove
    the ice and serve.

Care must be taken not to let the foam of the soda
water run over the glass while pouring it in. This
drink must be taken as soon as mixed, or it will lose
its flavor.

119. EAST INDIA COCKTAIL.
(Use a large bar glass.)

Fill the glass with shaved ice;
1 tea-spoonful of Curaçoa (red);
1 tea-spoonful of Pineapple syrup;
2 or 3 dashes of Bitters (Boker's genuine only);
2 dashes of Maraschino;
1 wine glass full of Brandy;
stir up with a spoon, strain into a cocktail glass,
twist a piece of lemon peel on top and serve.

This drink is a great favorite with the English
living in the different parts of East India.

120. SODA LEMONADE.
(Use a large bar glass.)

1 table-spoonful of sugar;
6 to 8 dashes of Lemon juice;
3 or 4 lumps of broken ice;
1 bottle of plain soda water;
stir up well with a spoon remove the ice and serve.

Open the soda beneath the counter, to avoid squirt-
ing part of it over the customer.

121. OLD STYLE WHISKEY SMASH.
(Use an extra large Whiskey glass.)

$^1/_4$ table-spoonful of sugar;
$^1/_2$ wine glass of water;
3 or 4 sprigs of mint, dissolve well;
fill the glass with small pieces of ice;
1 wine glass of Whiskey;
Put in fruit in season, mix well, place the strainer in the glass and serve.

122. SODA COCKTAIL.
(Use a large bar glass.)

4 or 5 lumps of broken ice;
5 or 6 dashes of Bitters (Boker's genuine only);
1 or 2 slices of Orange;
fill up the glass with Lemon soda water, and place a tea-spoon filled with sugar on top of the glass for the customer to put it in himself.

Do not let the foam of the soda spread over the glass in mixing the drink.

123. HOW TO MIX TOM AND JERRY.
(Use a punch bowl for the mixture.)

Use eggs according to quantity. Before using eggs, be careful and have them fresh and cold; go to work and take two bowls, break up your eggs very carefully, without mixing the yolk with the whites, but have the whites in a separate bowl, take an egg beater and beat the white of the eggs in such a manner, that it becomes a stiff froth: add, $1^1/_2$ table-spoonfuls of sugar for each egg, and mix this thoroughly together, and then beat the yolks of the eggs, until they are as thin as water; mix the yolks of the eggs with the whites and sugar together, until the mixture gets the consistency of a light batter, and it is necessary to stir the mixture up every little while to prevent the eggs from separating.

124. HOW TO DEAL OUT TOM AND JERRY.
(Take either a Tom and Jerry mug, or a bar glass.)

2 table-spoonfuls of the above mixture;
1 wine glass of Brandy;
1 pony glass of Jamaica rum;
fill the mug or glass with hot water or hot milk,
and stir up well with a spoon, then pour the
mixture from one mug to the other, three or four
times, until the above ingredients are thoroughly
mixed, grate a little nutmeg on top, and serve.

125. EGG LEMONADE.
(Use a large bar glass.)

1 fresh egg;
1 table-spoonful of sugar;
7 or 8 dashes of Lemon juice;
$^3/_4$ glass of fine ice;
Fill the balance up with water;
shake up in a shaker, until all the ingredients are
well mixed; then strain it into a large bar glass,
and serve.

This is a delicious summer drink of Americans,
and is also fancied by the Ladies.

126. ST. CROIX SOUR.
(Use a large bar glass.)

$^1/_2$ table-spoonful of sugar;
3 or 4 dashes of Lemon juice;
1 squirt Syphon Selters water, dissolve well with
a spoon;
$^3/_4$ glass of fine shaved ice;
1 wine glass of St. Croix rum;
mix well, place your seasonable fruit in a sour glass
and strain the above ingredients into the fruit, and
serve.

PLATE No. 6.

Kirschwasser or Brandy.

Annisette.

Chartreuse (yellow).

Curacoa (red).

BRANDY SHAMPERELLE.

Cognac.

Chartreuse (yellow).

Curacoa (red).

Vanilla (green).

Maraschino.

Parfait d'Amour, or Raspberry Syrup.

Cognac.

Vanilla (green).

Yolk of Egg.

Maraschino.

POUSSE CAFE.   POUSSE L'AMOUR.

127. EGG MILK PUNCH.

(Use a large bar glass.)

1 fresh egg;
$^3/_4$ table-spoonful of sugar;
$^1/_4$ glass of fine shaved ice;
1 wine glass of Brandy;
1 pony glass of St. Croix rum;
fill up the balance with good milk, shake the ingredients together until they become a stiff cream; strain into a large bar glass; grate a little nutmeg on top, and serve.

128. WHISKEY COBBLER.

(Use a large bar glass.)

$^1/_2$ table-spoonful of sugar;
$1^1/_2$ tea-spoonfuls of Pineapple syrup;
$^1/_2$ wine glass of Water or Selters, dissolve well
    with a spoon;
Fill up the glass with fine ice;
1 wine glass of Whiskey;
stir up well with a spoon, and ornament on top with grapes, oranges, pineapple and berries in season, and serve with a straw.

129. SHERRY AND EGG.

(Use a Whiskey glass.)

In preparing the above drink, place a small portion of Sherry wine into the glass, barely enough to cover the bottom, to prevent the egg, from sticking to the glass, then break an ice cold egg into it, hand this out to the customer and also the bottle of Sherry wine to help himself.

It is always proper to ask the customer whether he wishes the yolk only or the entire egg.

180. ST. CROIX CRUSTA.
(Use a large bar glass.)

Take a nice clean lemon, the same size as your wine glass, cut off both ends, and peel it the same as you would an apple, put the lemon peel in the glass, so that it will line the entire inside of the glass, dip the edge of the glass and the lemon peel in pulverized sugar and mix as follows:

3 or 4 dashes of Orchard syrup;
1 dash of Bitters (Boker's genuine only);
$1/2$ glass of fine ice;
1 small dash of Lemon juice;
2 dashes of Maraschino;
1 wine glass of St. Croix rum;

mix well with a spoon, and strain into a wine glass, dress with small pieces of pineapple and strawberries, and serve.

131. RHINE WINE COBBLER.
(Use a large bar glass.)

$1^{1}/_2$ table-spoonfuls of sugar;
$1^{1}/_2$ wine glass of water, dissolve well with a spoon;
$1^{1}/_2$ wine glasses of Rhine wine;
Fill the glass with shaved ice;

stir up well with a spoon; ornament with grapes, orange, pineapple, strawberries, in season, and serve with a straw.

This is a fashionable German drink.

132. HOT SPICED RUM.
(Take a hot water glass.)

1 or 2 lumps of loaf sugar;
.$1/2$ tea-spoonful of mixed allspice; dissolve with a little hot water;
1 wine glass of Jamaica rum;

Fill up the balance of the glass with hot water, mix well and grate a little nutmeg on top, and serve.

If the customer requires a small portion of butter in the above drink, you should use only that which is perfectly fresh, as butter is very desirable in cases of sore throats and colds, and sometimes a little batter of the Tom and Jerry is required in this hot drink.

133. MAY WINE PUNCH.
(Use a large punch bowl.)

Take one or two bunches of Waldmeister or Woodruff, and cut it up in two or three lengths, place it into a large bar glass, and fill up the balance with French Brandy, cover it up and let it stand for two or three hours, until the essence of the Woodruff is thoroughly extracted; cover the bottom of the bowl with loaf sugar, and pour from
4 to 6 bottles of plain Soda water over the sugar; cut up 6 oranges in slices;
$1/2$ pineapple, and sufficient berries and grapes;
8 bottles of Rhine or Moselle wine;
1 bottle of Champagne;
then put your Woodruff and Brandy, etc., into the bowl, and stir up with a ladle, and you will have $2^1/_2$ to 3 gallons of excellent May Wine Punch; surround the bowl with ice, serve in a wine glass in such a manner that each customer will get a piece of all of the fruits contained in the punch.

134. WHISKEY COCKTAIL.
(Use a large bar glass.)

$3/_4$ glass of fine shaved ice;
2 or 3 dashes of Gum syrup;
$1^1/_2$ or 2 dashes of Bitters; (Boker's genuine only);
1 or 2 dashes of Curaçoa;
1 wine glass of Whiskey;
stir up well with a spoon and strain it into a cocktail glass and squeeze a piece of Lemon peel on top, and serve.

This drink is without doubt one of the most popular American drinks in existence.

185. COLD WHISKEY SLING.
(Use a small bar glass.)

1 tea-spoonful of sugar;
$^1/_2$ wine glass of water, dissolve well;
1 or two small lumps of ice;
1 wine glass of Whiskey;
mix well, grate a little nutmeg on top, and serve.

This is an old fashioned drink generally called for by old gentlemen.

136. JERSEY COCKTAIL.
(Use a large bar glass.)

$^1/_2$ table-spoonful of sugar
3 or 4 lumps of broken ice;
3 or 4 dashes of Bitters; (Boker's genuine only);
1 wine glass of good Cider;
mix well and strain into a cocktail glass, and twist a piece of Lemon peel on top.

This is a favorite drink with Jersey people.

137. KIRSCHWASSER PUNCH.
(Use a large bar glass.)

$^1/_2$ table-spoonful of sugar;
1 or 2 dashes of Lime or Lemon juice;
3 or 4 dashes of Chartreuse (yellow);
dissolve well with a little water;
Fill the glass with ice;
1$^1/_2$ wine glass of Kirschwasser;
mix well with a spoon, ornament the top with fruit in season, and serve with a straw.

138. ORANGE LEMONADE.
(Use a large bar glass.)

1 table-spoonful of sugar;
1 dash at Lemon juice, squeeze out the juice of
    1 or 2 oranges;
Fill the glass with shaved ice;
Fill the balance with water, shake or stir well, and

dress the top with fruit in season, and serve with a straw.

This is a very delicious summer drink.

139. ARF AND ARF

(Use a large bar glass.)

The above is an old English drink, and has become quite a favorite in this country; it is mixed as follows:

$1/2$ glass of Porter and the other half glass of Ale; but in this country it is mostly understood to use half Old and half New Ale mixed; the proper way is, to ask how the customer desires it, and see that the drink if cold enough in summer time, but still not too cold.

140. LEMONADE.

(Use a large bar glass.)

$1^1/_2$ table-spoonful of sugar;
6 to 8 dashes of Lemon juice;
$^3/_4$ glass filled with shaved ice;
fill the balance with water; shake or stir well; dress with fruit in season, and serve with a straw.

To make this drink taste pleasant, it must be at all times good and strong; therefore take plenty of lemon juice and sugar.

141. PORT WINE SANGAREE.

(Use a small bar glass.)

1 tea-spoonful of sugar, dissolve well with a little
   water;
1 or 2 lumps of ice;
1 wine glass of Port wine;
stir up with a spoon, remove the piece of ice if required; grate a little nutmeg on top, and serve.

142. WHISKEY SOUR.
(Use a large bar glass.)

1/2 table-spoonful of sugar;
3 or 4 dashes of Lemon juice;
1 squirt of Syphon Selters water, dissolve the
   sugar and lemon well with a spoon;
Fill the glass with ice;
1 wine glass of Whiskey;
stir up well, strain into a sour glass; place your
fruit into it, and serve.

143. ST. CROIX FIX.
(Use a large bar glass.)

1/2 table-spoonful of sugar;
2 or 3 dashes of Lemon juice;
1/2 pony glass of pineapple syrup;
1/2 wine glass of water, dissolve well with a spoon;
Fill up the glass with ice;
1 wine glass of St. Croix Rum;
stir up well, ornament the top with fruit in season,
and serve with a straw.

144. PORTER SANGAREE.
(Use a large bar glass.)

1/2 table-spoonful of sugar;
1 wine glass of water, dissolve the sugar well;
3 or 4 small pieces of broken ice;
Fill up the balance of the glass with Porter, mix
well with a spoon, remove the ice, grate a little
nutmeg on top, and serve.

Do not let the foam of the Porter spread over the
glass.

145. HOT LEMONADE.
(Use a large bar glass.

1 table-spoonful of sugar;
7 or 8 dashes of Lemon juice;
Fill up the glass with hot water; stir up with a
spoon, and serve.

It is always necessary to pour a little hot water into the glass at first and stir a little, to prevent the glass from cracking, and also place a little fine ice in a separate glass in case the drink should be too hot.

146. BRANDY SCAFFA.
(Use a Sherry glass.)

$1/_4$ Sherry glass of Raspberry syrup;
$1/_4$ Sherry glass of Maraschino;
$1/_4$ Sherry glass of Chartreuse (green);
top it off with Brandy, and serve.

This drink must be properly prepared to prevent the different colors from running into each other, each must appear separate.

147. HOT APPLE TODDY.
(Use a hot apple toddy glass.)

In mixing this drink, an extra-large hot water glass must be used. Mix as follows:

$1/_2$ medium-sized, well roasted apple;
$1/_2$ table-spoonful of sugar, dissolve well with a little hot water;
1 wine glass full of Old Apple Jack;
Fill the balance with hot water, mix well with a spoon, grate a little nutmeg on top and serve with a bar spoon.

If the customer desires the drink strained, use a fine strainer, such as used for milk punches; attention must be given while roasting the apples that they are not overdone, but done in a nice and juicy manner; use only apples of the finest quality.

148. MULLED CLARET AND EGG.
(Use a large bar glass.)

1 table-spoonful of sugar;
1 tea-spoonful of cloves and cinnamon mixed;
$1^1/_2$ wine glass of Claret wine;
pour this into a dish over the fire until boiling;

2 yolks of fresh eggs, beaten to a batter with a
little white sugar;
pour the hot wine over the eggs, stirring continually while doing so, grate a little nutmeg on top and
serve. Do not stir the eggs into the wine, as this
would spoil the drink.

149 CALIFORNIA SHERRY WINE COBBLER.
(Use a large bar glass.)

$^1/_2$ table-spoonful of sugar;
1 pony glass of Pineapple syrup, dissolve well in
a little water;
Fill the glass with ice;
$1^1/_2$ wine glass of California Sherry wine;
stir up well with a spoon; ornament the top in a
fancy manner with oranges, pineapple and berries,
top it off with a little Old Port wine, and serve with
a straw.

150. BRANDY FIZZ.
(Use a large bar glass.)

$^1/_2$ table-spoonful of sugar;
3 or 4 dashes of Lemon juice;
$^3/_4$ of a glass of fine ice;
1 wine glass of Brandy;
mix well with a spoon, strain into a fizz or sour
glass, fill with Vichy or Selters water and serve.

151. BISHOP.
(Use a large bar glass.)

1 table-spoonful of sugar;
2 dashes of Lime or Lemon juice;
$^1/_2$ Orange squeezed into it;
$^1/_2$ wine glass of water, dissolve well;
$^3/_4$ of a glass of fine shaved ice;
fill the balance with Burgundy;
flavor with a few drops of Jamaica rum; stir up
well with a spoon; dress the top with a little fruit
and serve with a straw.

PLATE No. 7.

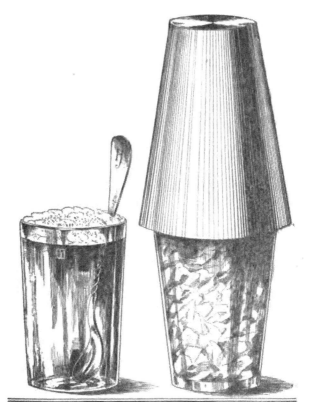

MORNING GLORY FIZZ.

152. ORCHARD PUNCH.
(Use a large bar glass.)

2 table-spoonfuls of Orchard syrup;
2 or 3 dashes of Lime or Lemon juice;
1/2 pony glass of Pineapple syrup, dissolve well
    with a little water;
fill the glass with fine ice;
1 wine glass full of California Brandy;
mix well with a spoon and ornament with grapes,
oranges, pineapple and berries; top off with a little
Port wine, and serve with a straw.

153. GIN AND TANSY.
(Use a Whiskey glass.)

I preparing this drink take a small bunch of tansy
and put it into an empty bottle or decanter; then
fill it up with good Old Holland Gin, and let it draw
sufficiently to get all the essence of the tansy into
the Gin. In serving this drink hand out the glass
and the bottle with the Gin and Tansy mixture. If
the mixture is too strong for the customers taste. let
him add a little more plain Gin to it.

154. JAMAICA RUM SOUR.
(Use a large bar glass.)

1/2 table-spoonful of sugar;
2 or 3 dashes of Lemon juice;
1 squirt of Syphon Selters, dissolve well;
3/4 glass of fine shaved ice;
1 wine glass of Jamaica rum;
stir well with a spoon, strain into a sour glass, ornament with fruit and serve.

155. PORT WINE FLIP.
(Use a large bar glass.)

1 fresh Egg;
1/2 tablespoonful of sugar;
3/4 glass of shaved ice;
1 wine glass of Port wine;

shake well in a shaker, strain into a wine glass, grate a little nutmeg on top, and serve.

156. HOT ARRAC PUNCH.
(Use a hot water glass.)

1 or 2 pieces of lump sugar dissolved in water;
3 or 4 drops of Lemon juice;
³/₄ wine glass of Arrac (Batavia);
fill the glass with hot water, stir well with a spoon, grate a little nutmeg on top and serve.

157. BRANDY SANGAREE.
(Use a small bar glass.)

1 or 2 lumps of ice;
¹/₂ wine glass of water;
¹/₂ table-spoonful of sugar;
1 glass of Brandy;
stir up well with a spoon; grate a little nutmeg on top, and serve; strain if desired.

158. GIN JULEP.
(Use a large bar glass.)

³/₄ table-spoonful of sugar;
3 or 4 sprigs of Mint;
¹/₂ wine glass of water, dissolve well, until the essence of the mint is extracted, then remove the mint;
fill up with fine ice;
1¹/₄ wine glass of Holland gin;
stir up well with a spoon, ornament it the same as you would Mint Julep, and serve.

159. HOT SCOTCH WHISKEY SLING.
(Use a hot water glass.)

1 piece of lump sugar;
³/₄ glass full of hot water;
1 piece of lemon peel;
1 wine glass of Scotch whiskey;
stir up well with a spoon, grate a little nutmeg on top, and serve.

160. SHERRY WINE AND BITTERS.
(Use a Sherry wine glass.)

In preparing this drink put in only 2 dashes of Bitters, (Boker's genuine only); and twist or turn the glass in such a manner, that the Bitters will line the entire inside of the glass; fill the glass up with Sherry wine and it will be mixed well enough to serve.

161. HOT MILK PUNCH.
(Use a large bar glass.)

1 table-spoonful of sugar;
$1/_4$ wine glass of St. Croix rum;
$3/_4$ wine glass of Brandy;
if desired use Jamaica rum instead of Brandy;
fill the glass with boiling hot milk;
stir up well with a spoon, grate a little nutmeg over it and serve.

In mixing this drink you must never use the shaker; if hot milk is not handy, use a tea-spoonful of condensed milk, and fill the balance with hot water; this will answer in place of hot milk.

162. GIN COCKTAIL.
(Use a large bar glass.)

Fill up the glass with ice;
2 or 3 dashes of Gum syrup;
2 or 3 dashes of Bitters, (Boker's genuine only);
1 dash of either Curaçoa or Absinthe;
1 wine glass of Holland gin;
stir up well, strain into a fancy cocktail glass, squeeze a piece of lemon peel on top, and serve.

Whether Curaçoa or Absinthe is taken depends on which the customer may desire.

163. TOM AND JERRY (COLD.)
(Use a Tom and Jerry mug, or a bar glass.)

This drink is prepared on the same principle as hot Tom and Jerry, with the exception of using cold water, or cold milk.

164. HOT WHISKEY.
(Use a hot Whiskey glass.)

Place a bar-spoon into the glass before pouring in hot water, to avoid cracking the glass, and have a separate glass filled with fine ice, which must be placed in a convenient position, so that if the customer finds his drink too hot, he can help himself to a little ice; the bartender should at all times handle the sugar with a pair of tongues. Mix as follows:
1 or 2 lumps of loaf sugar, with a little hot water
    to dissolve the sugar well;
1 wine glass of Scotch whiskey;
fill the glass with hot water; then mix well; squeeze and throw in the lemon peel, grate a little nutmeg on top and serve.

It is customary to use Scotch whiskey in preparing this drink, unless otherwise desired by the customer.

165. MEDFORD RUM PUNCH.
(Use a large bar glass.)

³/₄ table-spoonful of Sugar;
2 or 3 dashes of Lemon juice, dissolve well with
    a little water;
fill the glass with fine shaved ice;
1¹/₂ wine glass of Medford rum;
flavor with a few drops of Jamaica rum, stir up well and dress the top with fruit in season, and serve with a straw.

166. WHISKEY FIX.
(Use a large bar glass.)

¹/₂ table-spoonful of sugar;
2 or 3 dashes of Lime or Lemon juice, dissolve
    well with a little water;
¹/₂ pony glass of Pineapple syrup;
³/₄ glass of shaved ice;
1 wine glass of Whiskey;
stir up well with a spoon, and ornament with grapes, oranges, pineapple and berries; serve with a straw.

167. GIN SMASH.

(Use a large bar glass.)

$1/2$ table-spoonful of sugar;
2 or 3 sprigs of fresh mint, dissolve well with a
little water until the essence of the mint is
extracted;
$1/2$ glass of shaved ice;
1 wine glass of Holland gin;
stir up well with a spoon, strain into a sour glass,
ornament with a little fruit and serve.

168. HOT LOCOMOTIVE.

(Use a large bar glass.)

1 yolk of a raw egg;
$1/2$ table-spoonful of sugar;
1 pony glass of honey, dissolve well with a spoon;
$1^1/2$ wine glass full of Burgundy or Claret;
$1/2$ pony glass of Curaçoa;
put all the ingredients into a dish and put it over
a fire until it boils up, then pour from one mug to
the other for three or four times in succession; put
a slice of lemon into it, sprinkle with a little cinnamon and serve.

169. WHISKEY FIZZ.

(Use a large bar glass.)

$1/2$ tablespoonful of sugar;
2 or 3 dashes of Lemon juice, dissolve with a squirt
of Selters water;
fill the glass with ice;
1 wine glass of Whiskey;
stir up well, strain into a good sized fizz glass; fill
the balance up with Selters or Vichy water and serve.
This drink must be drank as soon as mixed, in
order not to lose its flavor.

170. STONE WALL.
(Use a large bar glass.)

$^1/_4$ table-spoonful of sugar;
3 or 4 lumps of ice;
1 wine glass of whiskey;
1 bottle of plain Soda water;
stir up well with a spoon, remove the ice and serve.
This is a very cooling drink, and generally called
for in the warm season.

171. HOT RUM.
(Use a hot water glass.)

1 or 2 lumps of loaf sugar, dissolve with a little
    hot water;
1 wine glass of Jamaica rum;
fill the balance with hot water, stir up well with a
spoon, grate a little nutmeg on top and serve.
The genuine Jamaica rum only should be used, in
order to make this drink palatable.

172. WINE LEMONADE.
(Use a large bar glass.)

1 table-spoonful of sugar;
5 or 6 dashes of Lemon juice;
fill up the glass with fine ice;
1 wine glass of wine, either Sherry, Claret or Port
    wine, whichever may be desired;
fill up the balance with water, shake well and dress
the top with fruit; serve with a straw.
    This is a favorite drink in Italy.

173. HOT IRISH WHISKEY PUNCH.
(Use a hot water glass.)

1 or 2 lumps of loaf sugar;
1 squirt of Lemon juice, dissolve in a little hot
    water;
1 wine glass of Irish whiskey;
fill the glass with hot water, stir up well, put a slice

of lemon into it, grate a little nutmeg on top and serve.

174. STONE FENCE.
(Use a Whiskey glass.)

1 wine glass of Whiskey;
2 or 3 lumps of broken ice;
fill the glass with cider, stir up well and serve.

175. SHERRY WINE SANGAREE.
(Use a Whiskey glass.)

1 tea-spoonful of sugar, dissolve well with a little
    water; '
1 or 2 lumps of broken ice;
1 wine glass of Sherry wine;
stir up well with a spoon, remove the ice, grate a
little nutmeg on top and serve.

176. OLD TOM GIN COCKTAIL.
(Use a large bar glass.)

Fill the glass with fine shaved ice;
2 or 3 dashes of Gum syrup;
1 or 2 dashes of Bitters (Boker's genuine only);
1 or 2 dashes of Curaçoa or Absinthe, if required;
1 wine glass of Old Tom gin;
stir up well with a spoon, strain into a cocktail glass,
twist a piece of Lemon peel on top, and serve.

177. GIN TODDY.
(Use a Whiskey glass.)

1/2 tea-spoonful of sugar, dissolve well in a little
    water;
1 or 2 lumps of broken ice;
1 wine glass of Holland gin;
stir up well and serve.
The proper way to serve this drink, is to dissolve
the sugar with a little water, put the spoon and ice
in the glass, and hand out the bottle of liquor to the
customer to help himself.

178. SODA AND NECTAR.
(Use a large bar glass.)

3 or 4 dashes of Lemon juice;
³/₄ of a glass of water;
¹/₂ tea-spoonful of bicarbonate of soda, with sufficient white sugar to sweeten nicely;
When mixed, put in the plain soda, stir well, and drink while in a foaming state.
This is an excellent morning drink to regulate the bowels.

179. GIN AND MOLASSES.
(Use a Whiskey glass.)

Pour into the glass a small quantity of Gin, to cover the bottom of it, then take one table-spoonful of New Orleans black molasses, and hand with a bar-spoon, and the bottle of Gin to the customer to help himself.
Hot water must be used to clean the glass afterwards, as it will be impossible to clean it in any other way.

180. FANCY BRANDY SOUR.
(Use a large bar glass.)

¹/₂ table-spoonful of sugar;
2 or 3 dashes of Lemon juice;
1 squirt of Syphon Selters water, dissolve the sugar and lemon well with a spoon;
Fill up the glass with ice;
1 wine glass of Brandy;
stir up well, place the fruits into the fancy sour glass, strain the ingredients into it, and serve.
(See Illustration, plate No. 11.)

181. PORT WINE COBBLER.
(Use a large bar glass.)

¹/₂ table-spoonful of sugar;
1 pony glass of Orchard syrup;
¹/₂ wine glass of water, dissolve well with a spoon;

PLATE No. 8.

CHAMPAGNE COBBLER.   MINT JULEP.

Fill the glass with fine ice;
1¹/₂ wine glass of Port wine;
mix up well, and ornament with grapes, berries etc.,
in season, and serve.

182. ROCK AND RYE.
(Use a Whiskey glass.)

This drink must be very carefully prepared, and
care must be taken to procure the best Rock Candy
syrup, and also the best of Rye Whiskey, as this
drink is an effective remedy for sore throats, etc.

In serving Rock and Rye, put ¹/₂ table-spoonful
of Rock Candy syrup into the glass, place a spoon
in it, and hand the bottle of Rye whiskey to the
customer, to help himself.

183. GIN SOUR.
(Use a large bar glass.)

¹/₂ table-spoonful of sugar;
2 or 3 dashes of Lemon juice;
1 dash of Lime juice;
1 squirt of Syphon Selters water;
dissolve the sugar and lemon well with a spoon;
³/₄ filled with fine shaved ice;
1 wine glass of Holland gin;
mix well, strain it into a sour glass, dress with a
little fruit in season, and serve.

184. PEACH AND HONEY.
(Use a small bar glass.)

1 table-spoonful of Honey;
1 wine glass of Peach Brandy;
stir well with a spoon and serve.

This drink is a great favorite in winter, and was
formerly called for as often as Rye and Rock is now.

6

185. SHERRY WINE EGG NOGG.
(Use a large bar glass.)

1 fresh egg,
$^1/_2$ table-spoonful of sugar;
Fill up the glass with fine ice;
1 pony glass of Brandy;
1 wine glass of Sherry wine;
shake the above ingredients well, until they are
thoroughly mixed together; strain it into a fancy
bar glass, large enough to hold the mixture; grate
a little nutmeg on top, and serve.

186. HOT BRANDY SLING.
(Use a hot water glass.)

1 lump of sugar, dissolve well with a little hot
    water;
1 wine glass of Brandy;
fill up with hot water, stir up with a spoon, grate
a little nutmeg on top and serve.
    If the customer desires it, cut a slice of lemon
into this drink.

187. MEDFORD RUM SMASH.
(Use a large bar glass.)

$^1/_2$ table-spoonful of sugar;
$^1/_2$ wine glass of water;
2 or 3 sprigs of mint; dissolve well the sugar with
    the mint, so that the essence of the same is
    well extracted;
$^1/_2$ glass of fine ice;
1 wine glass of old Medford rum;
stir well with a spoon, place the fruit into a sour
glass, and strain the above ingredients into it, and
serve.

188. GIN FIX.
(Use a large bar glass.)

$^1/_2$ table-spoonful of sugar;
3 or 4 dashes of Lime or Lemon juice;

$^1/_2$ pony glass of Pineapple syrup; dissolve well
    with a little water;
Fill up the glass with shaved ice;
1 wine glass of Holland gin;
stir up well with a spoon, ornament the top with
fruit in season, and serve with a straw.

189. COLD BRANDY TODDY.
(Use a Whiskey glass.)

$^1/_2$ teaspoonful of sugar;
$^1/_2$ wine glass of water, dissolve well with a spoon;
1 or 2 lumps of broken ice;
1 wine glass of Brandy;
stir up well, remove the ice, and serve.
    It is proper to dissolve the sugar with the water,
and hand the bottle of liquor, and glass and spoon
to the customer to help himself.

190. GIN AND WORMWOOD.
(Use a small bar glass.)

Take six to eight sprigs of wormwood, put these
in a quart bottle and fill up with Holland gin, leave
this stand for a few days, until the essence of the
wormwood is extracted into the gin. In handing
out this, pour a little of the above into a small
whiskey glass and hand it with the bottle of gin to
the customer to help himself
    This drink is popular in the eastern part of the
country, where the wormwood is used as a substitute
for bitters.

191. BOTTLE OF COCKTAIL FOR PARTIES.

1 qt. of good old Whiskey; providing the bottle
    is large enough;
1 pony glass of Curaçoa (red);
1 wine glass of Gum syrup;
$^3/_4$ pony glass of Bitters (Boker's genuine only);
mix this well by pouring it from one shaker into

another, until it is thoroughly mixed, pour it into a
bottle and cork it, and put a nice label on it, and
you will have an elegant bottle of Cocktail.

192. CLARET AND CHAMPAGNE CUP A LA BRUNOW.

(Use a large punch bowl for a party of twenty.)

The following Claret and Champagne should
from its excellence be called the Nectar of the
Czar, as it is so highly appreciated in Russia,
where for many years it has enjoyed a high reputation amongst the aristocracy of the Muscovite
Empire. Proportions:

3 bottles of Claret;
²/₃ pint of Curaçoa;
1 pint of Sherry;
1 pint of Brandy;
2 wine glasses of ratafia of raspberries;
3 oranges and one lemon cut in slices;
Some sprigs of green balm, and of borage;
2 bottles of German Selters water;
3 bottles of Soda water;

stir this together, and sweeten with capillaire
pounded sugar, until it ferments; let it stand one
hour; strain it and ice it well; it is then fit for use;
serve it in small glasses. The same for Champagne
cup; Champagne instead of Claret; Noyan instead
of ratafia. This quantity for an evening party of
twenty persons, for a smaller number reduce the
proportions.

193. BOMBAY PUNCH.

(Use a large bowl.)

Rub the sugar over the Lemons, until it has
absorbed all the yellow part of the skins of 6
Lemons, then put in the punch bowl:

1 lb. of loaf sugar;
2 bottles of imported Selters water;
1 Pineapple, cut up into slices;

6 Oranges, cut up into slices;
1 box of Strawberries;
2 Lemons, cut up in slices; mix well with a spoon,
and add
4 bottles of Champagne;
1 bottle of Brandy;
1 bottle of Pale Sherry,
1 bottle of Madeira wine;
1 gill of Maraschino;
stir up well with a spoon or ladle, and surround
the bowl with ice; serve it into a wine glass in
such a manner, that each customer will have a
piece of the above fruit.

194. PRUSSIAN GRANDEUR PUNCH.
(Use a large bowl.)

$1^1/_2$ lb. of loaf sugar;
6 Lemons, cut in slices;
1 gill of Anisette;
1 bottle Berlin Kümmel;
6 Oranges sliced;
1 bottle of Kirschwasser;
$^1/_2$ gallon of water;
6 bottles of Nordhauser Brantwein;
1 gill of Curaçoa;
stir up well with a punch ladle, and surround the
bowl with ice, and serve in a wine glass.

195. EMPIRE PUNCH.
(Use an extra large bowl.)

Rub the peel of 4 fine lemons, and also the peel
of two oranges, until it has absorbed all the yellow
part of the lemon and orange.
$1^1/_2$ lb. of lump sugar;
1 Pineapple, cut in slices;
12 fine oranges, cut in slices;
1 box of Strawberries;

2 bottles Apollinaris water; mix the above ingredients well with a ladle, and add
1/2 gill of Maraschino;
1/2 gill of Curaçoa;
1/2 gill of Benedictine;
1/2 gill of Jamaica rum;
1 bottle of Brandy;
6 bottles of Champagne;
4 bottles of Tokay wine;
2 bottles of Madeira;
4 bottles of Chateau Lafltte;
and mix this well with a large ladle, then strain
through a very fine sieve into a clean bowl and
surround the bowl with ice, fill it up over the edge
of the bowl, which will give it a beautiful appearance, and dress the edge with some leaves and
fruit, and ornament the punch in a fancy manner
with grapes, oranges, pineapple and strawberries.

196. HOT GIN SLING.
(Use a hot water glass.)

1 piece of loaf sugar, dissolve in a little water:
1 wine glass of Holland gin;
Fill up the balance with hot water;
stir with a spoon, and grate a little nutmeg on top,
and serve. Add a slice of lemon if the customer
desires it.

197. BRANDY DAISY.
(Use a large bar glass.)

1/2 table-spoonful of sugar;
2 or 3 dashes of Lemon juice;
1 squirt of Selters water, dissolve well with a
  spoon;
1/2 glass of Chartreuse (yellow);
Fill up the glass with fine ice;
1 glass of Brandy;
stir up well with a spoon, place the fruit into a
fancy bar glass, strain the ingredients into it, and
serve.

198. JAPANESE COCKTAIL.
(Use a large bar glass.)

$^3/_4$ glass of shaved ice;
2 or 3 dashes of Orgeat syrup;
2 or 3 dashes of Bitters (Boker's genuine only);
2 dashes of Maraschino;
1 glass of Eau Celeste (Himmels Wasser);
mix well with a spoon and strain it into a fancy
cocktail glass, twist a piece of lemon peel on top,
and serve.

199. SHANDY GAFF.
(Use a large bar glass or mug.)

Fill the glass half full of Old Ale or Bass Ale, and
the other half with Belfast Ginger Ale; stir up with
a spoon, and serve.

200. SARATOGA COCKTAIL.
(Use a large bar glass.

$^3/_4$ glass of fine shaved ice;
2 or 3 dashes of Pineapple syrup;
2 or 3 dashes of Bitters (Boker's genuine only);
2 or 3 dashes of Maraschino (di Zara);
$^3/_4$ glass of fine old Brandy;
mix well with a bar spoon and place 2 or 3 strawberries in a fancy cocktail glass, strain it, twist
a piece of lemon peel over it, top it off with 1
squirt of Champagne, and serve.

201. HOW TO SERVE A PONY GLASS OF BRANDY.
(Use a pony glass.)

In serving this drink hand out the pony glass
filled with Brandy, also a whiskey glass, into which
the brandy is emptied, a glass of ice water, and a
little separate ice to cool the brandy; the latest style
of serving a pony of brandy, is to place the pony
at the edge of the counter, then take a whiskey

tumbler upside down in the left hand, and place it over the pony glass of brandy, then reverse the glass, as well as the pony glass containing the brandy, so as to have the stem of the pony glass on top, and the brandy at the bottom of the whiskey glass, in order to be convenient for the customer. (See Illustration, plate No. 2).

202. BLACK STRIPE.
(Use a large bar glass.)

1 wine glass of St. Croix rum;
1 table-spoonful of molasses;
This drink can be made either in summer or winter; if in the former season, mix one table-spoonful of water and cool with shaved ice; if in the latter, fill up the glass with boiling water; use only the best New Orleans molasses, and grate a little nutmeg on top.

203. SOLDIERS CAMPING PUNCH.

Boil a large kettle of strong black coffee, take a large dish and put 4 pounds of lump sugar into it; then pour 4 bottles of brandy and 2 bottles of Jamaica rum over the sugar, and set it on fire, let the sugar dissolve and drop into the black coffee; stir this well and you will have a good hot punch for soldiers on guard.

204. GIN AND CALAMUS.
(Use a Whiskey glass.)

In preparing this drink, take 3 or 4 long pieces of calamus root, cut it in small pieces and put into an empty bottle; fill up the bottle with gin, and let it draw sufficiently to get all the essence of the calamus into the gin.

In serving this drink, hand out the whiskey glass, and the bottle with the gin and calamus mixture, to let the customer help himself.

If the mixture in the bottle should be too strong for the customer, let him add plain gin to suit his taste.

205. ORGEAT LEMONADE.

(Use a large bar glass.)

$1^1/_2$ wine glass of Orgeat syrup;
$1/_2$ table-spoonful of sugar;
6 to 8 dashes of Lemon juice;
$3/_4$ glass of shaved ice;
fill the glass with water;
mix up well and ornament with grapes, berries, etc.,
in season, and serve with a straw.
This is a fine drink in warm climates.

206. BEEF TEA.

(Use a hot water glass.)

$1/_4$ tea-spoonful of the best Beef Extract;
fill the glass with hot water;
stir up well with a spoon, and hand this to the
customer, place pepper, salt and celery salt handy,
and if the customer should require it, put in a small
quantity of Sherry wine or Brandy.

207. GIN AND MILK.

(Use a Whiskey glass.)

Hand the bottle of Gin, glass and spoon out to the
customer to help himself, fill up the balance with
good, rich ice cold milk, stir up with a spoon and
you will have a very nice drink.

208. COLUMBIA SKIN.

(Use a small bar glass.)

1 tea-spoonful of sugar, dissolve well with a little
    water;
1 slice of Lemon;
2 or 3 pieces of broken ice;
1 wine glass of rum;
stir up well with a spoon; grate a little nutmeg on
top and serve.
This drink is called Columbia Skin by the Boston
people.

209. BRANDY STRAIGHT.
(Use a Whiskey glass.)

Hand out the glass with the bottle of Brandy to the customer, also a glass of ice water; as Brandy is never kept on ice the bartender should put a piece of ice in the glass; it is not pleasant to drink when warm; do the same with all other liquors that are not kept on ice.

210. CLARET COBBLER.
(Use a large bar glass or goblet.)

1 table-spoonful of Orchard syrup;
$1/2$ table-spoonful of sugar;
$1/4$ of an orange;
1 squirt of Selters water; dissolve well with a spoon;
fill with fine shaved ice;
$1^1/2$ wine glass of good Claret wine;
stir well and ornament with slices of orange, pineapple, lemon, etc., and serve.

211. MILK AND SELTERS.
(Use a medium sized bar glass.)

In serving this drink, which is strictly temperance, it is proper for the bartender to half fill the glass with Selters, and the rest with milk; if it is done otherwise you will have nothing but foam in your glass, which would cause delay if a party has to be attended to.

212. WHISKEY AND CIDER.
(Use a Whiskey glass.)

Hand the bottle of whiskey to the customer to help himself, fill up the glass with good apple cider, stir well with a spoon, and serve, and you will have a very nice drink.

The author recommends good apple cider in preference to pear, or any other kind of fruit cider.

213. CHAMPAGNE VELVET.

(Use a large sized goblet.

For this drink a bottle of Champagne and a bottle of Irish Porter must be opened. It is mixed as follows:
Fill the glass $1/2$ full with Porter, the balance with Champagne;
stir up with a spoon slowly, and you have what is called Champagne Velvet, because it will make you feel within a short time as fine as silk.
It is rather an expensive drink, but a good one.

214. BURNT BRANDY AND PEACH.

(Use a small bar glass.)

This drink is a very popular one in the Southern States, where it is frequently used as a cure for diarrhœa.
1 wine glass of Cognac;
$1/2$ table-spoonful of white sugar, burned in a saucer or plate;
2 or 3 slices of dried peaches;
place the dried fruit into a glass and pour the liquor over them, grate a little nutmeg on top and serve.

215. RHINE WINE AND SELTERS.

(Use a large wine glass.

The bartenders attention is called to the fact, that when a customer calls for Rhine wine and Selters water, he desires a larger portion of wine than of Selters; and if he should call for Selters and wine, he desires more Selters than wine; attention must be paid that both the wine and the Selters are continually kept on ice.
This is a favorite drink with German people, and preferred by them in many cases to lemonade.

216. BRANDY AND GINGER ALE.
(Use a large bar glass.)

2 or 3 lumps of broken ice;
1 wine glass of Brandy;
1 bottle of good Ginger ale;
mix well together; particular attention must be paid when pouring the ginger ale into the other mixtures, not to let the foam run over the glass, and it is proper to ask the customer whether he desires imported or domestic ale; the imported being the best to use, as it mixes better, and will give better satisfaction than the domestic.

217. SHERRY WINE AND ICE.
(Use a Whiskey glass.)

1 or 2 lumps of broken ice;
place a bar-spoon into the glass, hand this out with the bottle of Sherry wine, and let the sustomer help himself.

If a hotel, restaurant or café is attached to the establishment, and the customer should call for such drink at the table, it is the bartenders duty to fill the glass with Sherry wine, and not send the bottle to the table, unless requested to do so.

218. BRANDY AND SODA.
(Use a large bar glass.)

3 or 4 lumps of broken ice;
1 wine glass of Brandy;
1 bottle of plain soda water;
mix well with a spoon, but attention must be paid not to let the mixture spread over the glass.

This is a delicious drink in summer and fancied very much by English people, and is also called Brandy Split by them.

219. SARATOGA BRACE UP.
(Use a large bar glass.)

1 table-spoonful of white sugar;
2 or 3 dashes of Bitters (Boker's genuine only);

2 or 3 dashes of Lemon juice
1 dash of Lime juice;
2 dashes of Anisette;
1 fresh egg;
³/₄ glass of Brandy;
¹/₂ glass of shaved ice;
shake this up thoroughly in a shaker, strain it into
a large sized bar glass, and fill with Syphon Vichy
or Apollinaris water and serve.

220. BRANDY AND·GUM.
(Use a Whiskey glass.)

3 or 4 dashes of gum;
1 or 2 pieces of broken ice;
place a bar spoon into the glass, and hand this with
a bottle of brandy to the customer to help himself.

When any other liquor is called for, it is served
in the same manner.

221. IMPERIAL BRANDY PUNCH.
(For a party of twenty.)

1 gallon of water;
3 quarts of Brandy;
1 pint of Jamaica rum;
1¹/₂ lbs. of white sugar;
juice of 6 lemons;
3 oranges sliced;
1 pineapple, pared and cut up;
1 gill of Curaçoa;
2 gills of raspberry syrup;
Ice, and berries in season;
mix well together in a large bowl, and you will have
a splendid punch.

If not sweet enough, add more sugar.

222. THE AMERICAN CHAMPAGNE CUP.
(Use a large punch bowl for a party of forty.)

2 wine glasses of Pineapple syrup;
4 to 6 sprigs of green balm;

1 quart of Curaçoa (red);
1 pint of Chartreuse (green);
1 quart of fine old Brandy or Cognac·
1 quart of Tokay wine;
4 bottles of Apollinaris water;
6 Oranges, cut in slices;
2 Lemons, cut in slices;
stir up well together, let it stand two hours, strain
it into another bowl and add:
  ¹/₂ Pineapple cut in slices·
  ¹/₂ box of Strawberries;
  6 bottles of Champagne;
Place the bowl in the ice, ana sweeten with a little
sugar and let it ferment, stir up well and serve the
same as American Claret Cup, and this will give
satisfaction to any Bon Ton party in America.

223. FINE LEMONADE FOR PARTIES.
(Use a punch bowl—1 gallon.)

Take the rind of 8 lemons:
juice of 12 lemons;
2 lbs. of loaf sugar;
1 gallon of boiling water;
rub the rinds of the 8 lemons on the sugar until
it has absorbed all the oil from them, and
put it with the remainder of the sugar into a jug;
add the lemon juice and pour the boiling water over
the whole. When the sugar .is dissolved, strain
the lemonade through a piece of muslin, and when
cool, it will be ready for use. The lemonade will
be much improved by having the whites of 4 eggs
beaten up with it. A larger or smaller quantity
of this lemonade may be made by increasing or
diminishing the quantity of the ingredients.

224. WHITE PLUSH.
(Use a small bar glass.)

Hand a bottle of Bourbon or Rye whiskey to
the customer and let him help himself. Fill up the

glass with fresh milk. This is what is called White
Plush, it has been an old time drink known for
many years.

225. ENGLISH BISHOP.

(Use a small punch bowl to make 1 quart.)

1 quart of Port wine;
1 Orange (stuck pretty well with cloves, the
    quantity being a matter of taste);
roast the orange before a fire, and when sufficiently
brown, cut in quarters, and pour over it a quart
of Port Wine, (previously made hot), add sugar
to taste, and let the mixture simmer over the fire
for half an hour.

226. BRANDY SHRUB.

(Use bowl—to make six quarts.)

4 lbs. of loaf sugar, dissolve well with a bottle
    of plain soda water;
4 quarts of old Brandy;
2 quarts of Sherry wine;
10 lemons;
peel the rinds of 4 lemons; add the juice of the
other 6 lemons and mix with brandy into the bowl,
cover it close for 5 days, then add the Sherry wine
and sugar, strain through a bag, and bottle it.
This also applies to all the other Shrubs.

227. CRIMEAN CUP A LA MARMORA.

(Use a bowl for mixing.)

1 pint of Orgeat syrup;
$1/2$ pint of Cognac brandy;
$1/4$ pint of Maraschino;
$1/4$ pint of Jamaica rum;
1 bottle of Champagne;
1 bottle of Soda Water;
3 ounces of sugar;
2 Lemons, cut in slices;

2 Oranges, cut in slices;
and a few slices of Pineapple;
stir up well with a spoon or ladle, then place it into
your dish filled with ice, and serve.

228. CLARET CUP FOR A PARTY.
(Use a bowl for mixing.)

8 to 12 pieces of lump sugar;
1 bottle of Apollinaris water;
2 Lemons, cut in slices;
2 Oranges, cut in slices;
1/2 Pineapple, cut in slices;
2 wine glasses of Maraschino;
mix well with a ladle, place this into your vessel
or tin dish filled with ice, then when the party is
ready to call for it, add
4 bottles of very fine Claret;
1 bottle of Champagne, or any other sparkling
   wine;
mix thoroughly and place sufficient berries on top
and serve it into a fancy wine glass, and you will
have an elegant Claret Cup.

229. RASPBERRY SHRUB.
(Use a bowl for mixing.)

1 quart of Vinegar;
3 quarts of ripe Raspberries;
after standing a day, strain it, adding to each pint
a pound of sugar, and skim it clear, while boiling
about half an hour.

Put a wine glass of brandy to each pint of the
shrub, when cool.

2 spoonfuls of this mixed with a tumbler of water,
is an excellent drink in warm weather and during
a fever.

230. CURRANT SHRUB.
(Use a bowl for mixing; general rule for preparing.)

1 quart of strained currant juice;
1 1/2 lbs. of loaf sugar;
boil it gently 8 or 10 minutes, skimming it well;

FANCY BRANDY SMASH.

take it off, and when lukewarm, add $^1/_2$ gill of brandy to every pint of shrub. Bottle tight.

A little shrub mixed with ice water makes a delicious drink. Shrub may be made of Cherry or Raspberry juice by this method, but the quantity of sugar must be reduced.

231. PUNCH A LA FORD.
(For bottling.)

3 dozen Lemons;
1 pint of Cognac;
2 lbs. of loaf sugar;
1 pint of Jamaica rum;

The lemons should have smooth rinds; peel the yellow rinds off quite thin with a sharp knife, place them in an earthen vessel; add the sugar, and stir thoroughly for nearly half an hour with a flat piece of wood to extract the essential oil. Pour on boiling water, and stir until the sugar is completely dissolved.

Cut and squeeze the lemon, straining the juice from the pits. Place the pits in a jug and pour boiling water upon them to obtain the mucilage in which they are enveloped. Pour $^1/_2$ of the lemon juice into the syrup, strain the water from the pits, and add it also to the syrup, taking care that the syrup is not too watery.

Next, add more sugar or lemon juice, to make the mixture according to taste.

Lastly, add and stir in the above amount of spirits into every 3 qts. of lemonade, and bottle.

This punch improves by age, if kept in a cool cellar.

232. ORANGE PUNCH.

$^3/_4$ pint of Rum;
$^3/_4$ pint of Brandy;
$^1/_2$ pint of Porter;
$3^1/_2$ pints of boiling water;

7

$^3/_4$ lb. of loaf sugar;
4 Oranges.
Infuse the peel of 2, and the juice of 4 oranges
with the sugar in the water for $^1/_2$ hour; strain, and
add the porter, rum and brandy. Sugar may be
added, if it is desired sweeter.
A liquor glass of Curaçoa, Noyeau, or Maraschino
is considered an improvement.
Instead of using both, rum and brandy, $1^1/_2$ pints
of either alone will answer.
This is also an excellent recipe for Lemon Punch
by substituting lemons for oranges.

233. FEDORA.
(Use a large bar glass.)

1 pony of Brandy;
1 pony of Curaçoa;
$^1/_2$ pony of Jamaica rum;
$^1/_2$ pony of Bourbon;
1 table-spoonful of powdered sugar, dissolved in
    a little water;
1 slice of Lemon;
Fill the tumbler with fine ice; shake well and ornament with berries or small pieces of orange, serve
with a straw.

234. ROCHESTER PUNCH.
(For a small party.)

2 bottles of sparkling Catawba;
2 bottles of sparkling Isabella;
1 bottle of Sauterne;
2 wine glasses of Maraschino;
2 wine glasses of Curaçoa.
Flavor with ripe strawberries. Should strawberries
not be in season, add a few drops of extract of peach
or vanilla. Ice in a cooler.

235. DUKE OF NORFOLK PUNCH FOR BOTTLING.

20 qts, of French brandy;
30 Lemons;
30 Oranges;
30 qts. of cold boiled water;
15 lbs. of double refined sugar;
2 qts. of new milk.

Pare off the peel of the oranges and lemons very thin, excluding all the white rind. Infuse in the brandy for 12 hours. Dissolve the sugar in the water; add the juice of the oranges and of 24 of the lemons; pour this upon the brandy and peels, mixing it thoroughly. Strain through a very fine hair sieve into a barrel that has held spirits, and add the milk. Stir and bung close. After it has been six weeks in a warm cellar, bottle in perfectly clean and dry bottles, and cork well. This will keep for years and improve with age.

236. BISHOP A LA PRUSSE.

1 bottle of Claret;
1/2 lb. of pounded loaf sugar;
4 good sized bitter Oranges;

Roast the oranges until they are of a pale brown color; lay them in a tureen, and cover them with the sugar, adding 3 glasses of the Claret; cover the tureen and let it stand until the next day. When required for use, place the tureen in a pan of boiling water, press the oranges with a spoon, and run the juice through a sieve. Boil the remainder of the Claret; add the strained juice, and serve warm in glasses. Port wine may be substituted for Claret, and lemons may be used instead of oranges, but this is not often done when Claret is used.

237. COLD RUBY PUNCH.

1 quart of Batavia Arrac;
1 quart of Port wine;

3 pints of green tea;
1 pound of loaf sugar;
juice of 6 lemons;
$^1/_2$ pineapple cut in small slices;
Dissolve the sugar in the tea, add other materials
served iced.

. 238. ENGLISH CURACOA.

6 ounces of very thin orange peel;
1 pint of Whiskey;
1 pint of clarified syrup;
1 drachm powdered Alum;
1 drachm Carbonate of Potash;
Place the orange peel in a bottle, which will hold
a quart with the whiskey; cork tightly and let
the contents remain for 10 to 12 days, shaking the
bottle frequently. Then strain out the peel, add
the syrup; shake well, and let it stand for 3 days.
Take out a tea-cupful into a mortar, and beat up
with the alum and potash; when well mixed, pour
it back into the bottle, and let it remain for a week.
The Curaçoa will then be perfectly clear and equal
in flavor to the best imported article.

239. BOTTLED VELVET.
(Use a punch bowl.)

1 bottle of Moselle;
$^1/_2$ pint of Sherry;
2 table-spoonfuls of sugar;
1 lemon;
1 sprig of verbena;
peel the lemon very thin, using only sufficient of
the peel to produce the desired flavor; add the
other ingredients; strain and ice.

240. SODA NEGUS.
(Use a small punch bowl; about 1 quart.)

1 pint of Port wine;
12 lumps of white loaf sugar;
8 cloves;
grated nutmeg sufficient to fill a small tea-spoon;

put the above ingredients into a thoroughly clean
sauce pan, warm and stir them well, but do not
suffer it to boil; upon the warm wine empty a
bottle of plain soda water. This makes a delicious
and refreshing drink.

241. BALAKLAVA NECTAR.
(For a party of fifteen.)

Thinly peel the rind of $1/2$ lemon, shred it fine,
and put it in a punch bowl, add 4 table-spoonfuls of
crushed sugar and the juice of

1 lemon;
1 gill of Maraschino;
2 bottles of soda water;
2 bottles of Claret;
2 bottles of Champagne;

stir well together and dress the top with fruit in
season, and serve.

242. ENGLISH ROYAL PUNCH.
(Use a bowl for mixing for a small party.)

1 pint of hot green tea;
$1/2$ pint of Brandy;
$1/2$ pint of Jamaica rum;
1 wine glass of Curaçoa;
1 wine glass of Arrac;
juice of 2 Limes;
1 Lemon, cut in slices;
$1/2$ lb. of sugar;

mix this thoroughly with a ladle, and add:

4 Eggs, the white only, and drink this as hot as
   possible;

This composition is good enough for an Emperor
or King, and the materials are admirably blended;
the inebriating effects of the spirits being deadened
by the tea, whilst the eggs soften the mixture, and
destroy the acrimony of the acid and sugar. If the
punch is too strong, add more green tea to taste,
and if not hot enough, place the entire mixture over
the fire and have it heated, but not boiled, and serve.

Bedeutung der beibehaltenen englischen Ausdrücke.

Da einige der in der englischen Sprache gebräuchlichen technischen Ausdrücke sich nicht ohne Umschreibung Deutsch wiedergeben lassen, hat der Herausgeber dieselben beibehalten und deren Bedeutung in Nachfolgendem erklärt:

Bar. — Schenktisch, einschliesslich der Bank, der hinter demselben angebrachten Spiegel, etc., etc.

Counter. — Der vordere Theil der Bar; der eigentliche Schenktisch an dem Gäste bedient werden.

Bartender. — Die Person, welche die Bar verwaltet, sowie die Getränke zusammenstellt und verabreicht.

Bench. — Die unter dem Counter befindliche Abtheilung, worauf die zum Gebrauche nöthigen Sachen, wie Gläser, Flaschen, Eis- und Wasserbehälter, etc., gestellt werden.

Cooler. — Ein Kübel oder sonstiges Gefäss, um Weine, besonders Champagner, beim Serviren kalt zu stellen.

Dash — plural Dashes. — Damit wird dasjenige Quantum einer Flüssigkeit bezeichnet, welches durch eine einzige, kurze, rasche Bewegung einer Flasche entströmt, deren Kork oder Pfropfen mit einem feinen Röhrchen versehen ist.

Gigger. — Maassgefäss, mit welchem die zu den gemischten Getränken nöthigen Flüssigkeiten gemessen werden.

Skids. — Ein aus starken Balken gezimmertes Gestell, auf welchem die grösseren Fässer, Weine, Liqueure, Syrupe, Ale, Porter, etc. enthaltend, gelagert werden.

Mug. — Ein mit einem Henkel versehenes Trinkgefäss aus Metall, welches in früherer Zeit bei Engländern und Amerikanern sehr beliebt war, und aus welchem Ale und Porter getrunken wurden.

Mop. — Dieses ist ein Geräth zum Reinigen des Bodens und besteht aus langen gedrehten, zu einem Bündel gewundenen Baumwollfäden, versehen mit einem langen Stiel, um überall bequem beikommen zu können.

Neues und Verbessertes

Illustrirtes

Handbuch für Bartender,

— oder: —

Wie man Getränke mischt,

— enthaltend —

Practische Regeln, Winke und Anweisungen über sämmtliche
Bedürfnisse, gründliche Belehrung über alle Einzeln-
heiten des Geschäfts, vollkommene und correcte
Recepte aller gemischten Getränke der Jetztzeit
die in Amerika, England, Deutschland, Frank-
reich, Italien, Russland, Spanien und
anderen Ländern beliebt sind,

— sowie —

*Listen sämmtlicher Bar-Utensilien, Anweisungen zur richtigen
Behandlung von Liqueuren, Weine, Bier, Ale und Porter
in Fässern und Flaschen.*

HARRY JOHNSON,

Herausgeber und Professioneller Bartender,

— und —

Praktischer Lehrer der Bartender-Kunst,

NEW YORK.

ELECTROTYPED AND PRINTED BY I. GOLDMANN, 190 WILLIAM ST., N. Y.

VORREDE.

Indem ich nachstehendes Buch der Oeffentlichkeit übergebe, erlaube ich mir, dem werthen Leser einen kurzen Ueberblick meiner Thätigkeit zu unterbreiten.

Seit meiner frühesten Jugend im Hotelgeschäfte thätig, habe ich es durch Fleiss und Studium zu den ersten Stellen in den grössten und feinsten Hotels Amerika's gebracht, sowie alle bedeutenden Länder der Welt bereist, so dass ich von der Pike auf nunmehr mit allen Einzelheiten meines Geschäfts dermassen vertraut bin, dass ich mein Buch als vollendetstes Werk dem Publikum übergeben kann. Ich habe weder Mühe noch Kosten gescheut, mir Kenntnisse nach jeder Richtung anzueignen und solche immer wieder zu erweitern, habe ferner einen reichen Schatz von Erfahrungen zur Seite, welchen ich auch im Privatunterricht bereits mit vielem Erfolge verwerthete, indem sämmtliche meiner Schüler zu den anerkannt besten und ausgezeichnetsten Bartendern dieses Landes gehören, und bin nun nach reiflichem Studium in der Lage, diese meine Kenntnisse in diesem Buche allen Denen, die in meiner Branche wirken, nutzbar zu machen.

Ich beabsichtige, mit der Herausgabe dieses Buches es Jedermann zu ermöglichen, bei Verabreichung irgend eines gewünschten Getränkes den Geschmack des Gastes richtig zu treffen, indem meine Re-

cepte und Anweisungen wohl durchdacht sind und
auf meinen eigenen reichen Erfahrungen basiren.

Ich glaube mir kein ungerechtfertigtes Lob auszu-
sprechen, wenn ich nachstehendes Werk, dem ich
das Studium eines Lebensalters widmete, als ein
vollendetes bezeichne, und werden sich die Leser
desselben bald überzeugen, mit welcher besonderen
Genauigkeit und Correktheit alle nur irgend existi-
renden gemischten Getränke zusammengestellt sind.
Ausser den genauesten Recepten und Instructionen
für Zusammenstellung gemischter Getränke habe
ich nicht verfehlt, meinem Werke ein Verzeichniss
aller zur Einrichtung eines Hotels, Restauration
oder Bar nothwendigen Gegenstände, sowie aller
reinen Getränke einzuverleiben, und gebe ich mich
daher der angenehmen Hoffnung hin, allen An-
forderungen der Jetztzeit gerecht geworden zu sein.

Dieses Buch ist das erste und einzige Werk dieser
Art in deutscher Sprache und empfehle ich daher
dasselbe allen Hotel- und Restaurations-Besitzern
und Bartendern, sowie Allen, welche sich diesem
Geschäft widmen wollen, zur geneigten Beachtung.

Dieses Buch eignet sich auch für jeden Haushalt,
indem dessen Inhalt für jede Hausfrau von vielem
Nutzen und Werth sein wird.

Hochachtungsvoll,

HARRY JOHNSON.

Inhalts-Verzeichniss.

Liste der Utensilien, Weine, Liqueure, etc.
Von 44 bis 55.

Liste der "Mixed Drinks."
Von 56 bis 214.

Für Recepte, die im deutschen Theile dieses Buches nicht enthalten sind, sehe man das englische Inhaltsverzeichniss nach.

1. Allgemeine Anweisungen über das Benehmen und die Pflichten eines Bartenders.

Die erste Grundbedingung eines Bartenders ist Bescheidenheit und Zuvorkommenheit gegen die Gäste, und hat derselbe auf die an ihn gerichteten Fragen, seinem besten Wissen nach, deutlich und correkt zu antworten und niemals das grosse Wort zu führen, da sich nur dadurch ein Gast angezogen fühlen wird. Der Bartender darf eben nicht zu wenig, aber auch nicht zu viel sprechen, soll immer zuvorkommend sein und es dem Gaste im Locale möglichst angenehm und bequem machen. Einen Unterschied bei der Bedienung eines mehr oder minder bemittelten Gastes darf der Bartender niemals machen, da jeder Gast, der sich anständig benimmt, zu gleichem Entgegenkommen berechtigt ist und sich im entgegengesetzten Falle bewogen fühlen wird, das Local nicht mehr zu betreten. Der Bartender hat ferner besonders darauf zu achten, dass er stets elegant, rein und sauber gekleidet ist, da das Aeussere des Bartenders sehr viel Einfluss auf den Gast ausübt, indem Eleganz mit Reinlichkeit gepaart ungemein anzieht. Auch möge der Bartender nicht ausser Acht lassen, dass eine schöne und stramme Haltung zur Vollendung des Ganzen gehört. (Siehe Illustrationen, Platten 1 und 3.)

Wenn eine Anzahl Herren gleichzeitig an die Bar tritt, dann soll der Bartender erst jedem der Gäste ein Glas Eiswasser vorsetzen und sodann in höflichem Tone fragen, was die Herren zu trinken wünschen. Ferner ist es Pflicht des Bartenders, den Gast zu fragen, wie er das betreffende Getränk, wenn solches ein gemischtes ist, wünscht, ob stark oder schwach, mehr oder weniger süss oder sauer etc. Nach dem Wunsche des Gastes muss sich dann der Bartender beim Mischen des bestellten Getränkes richten. Die Mischung des betreffenden Getränkes muss mit möglichster Eleganz und Zierlichkeit oberhalb des Counters geschehen, damit der Gast sehen kann, wie es bereitet wird, und ist es für den Bartender besonders empfehlend, wenn er darin grosse Gewandtheit zeigen kann. In der Kunst, die Gäste gewandt und elegant zu bedienen, liegt oft das Geheimniss, welches dem Locale eine grosse Kundschaft sichert. Die zu verwendenden Gläser müssen stets rein und sauber geputzt sein, so dass kein Fleckchen daran haftet, und ist daher jedes Glas vom Bartender vor dem Gebrauche genau zu besichtigen. Wenn die Gäste die Bar verlassen haben, muss der Bartender die Gläser unverzüglich von dem Counter fortnehmen, und wenn Zeit dazu vorhanden ist, die gebrauchten Gläser sofort reinigen und an Ort und Stelle bringen.

Der Bartender muss ferner darauf sehen, die Bank (bench), (siehe Illustration, Platte 2), stets in strictester Ordnung zu haben, damit er Alles rasch und bequem bei der Hand hat, da ihm dies sein Geschäft sehr erleichtert, was sehr wichtig ist, weil seine Aufmerksamkeit stets überall hin gerichtet sein soll.

2. Praktische Winke und richtige Methode zur Anlernung eines Anfängers.

In den dreissig Jahren meiner Geschäftsthätigkeit, auf die ich, wie ich mir schmeicheln darf, mit Stolz zurückblicken kann, hatte ich Gelegenheit, Hunderte von jungen Leuten in das Geschäft einzuführen. Auf Grund meiner gesammelten Erfahrungen möchte ich mir nun erlauben, jedem Wirth, Manager oder Bartender den Rath zu ertheilen, den Anfänger strict zu behandeln, ihm gute Manieren beizubringen und das Augenmerk darauf zu richten, dass er weder gegen seine Vorgesetzten noch gegen die Gäste sich Freiheiten herausnimmt. Ferner ist es am Platze, dass man ihn über alle Besonderheiten und Eigenthümlichkeiten des Geschäfts genau informire, im

PLATE No. 10.

WHISKEY DAISY.

festem aber nicht unfreundlichem Tone mit ihm
rede und ihn möglichst wenig gemeine und
schlechte Redensarten hören lasse; auch sehe man
zu, dass er stets nett gekleidet ist und alle seine
Obliegenheiten auf's Stricteste erfülle, ohne dass
man ihm aber die Freiheit, die ihm zukommt,
beschränke. Auf diese Weise wird man aus ihm
einen sehr guten, brauchbaren und für das Geschäft
passenden jungen Mann machen. Vor Allem aber
ist es die heiligste Pflicht des Bartenders, dem jungen Mann stets ein gutes Beispiel zu geben, ihn
soviel wie irgend möglich auf Alles aufmerksam zu
machen, so dass er, wenn er zum Manne herange-
reift, sich selbst als einen vollkommenen Gentleman
betrachten darf und nicht nöthig hat, seines Geschäftes sich zu schämen. Allerdings giebt es,
wie ich leider bekennen muss, viele Leute, welche
die Meinung haben, in unserem Geschäft gäbe es
keine Gentlemen; würden aber diese das Wesen
unseres Geschäftes gründlich kennen und mit einem
der vielen tüchtigen Geschäftsleute unserer Branche
bekannt sein, so würden sie sehr bald zur der Ueber-
zeugung gelangen, dass unser Geschäft, wenn es
richtig und systematisch betrieben werden soll unbedingt einen Gentleman erfordert. Freilich gegen
die Gewohnheit beschränkter Köpfe, keinen Unterschied zu machen, kann man nicht ankämpfen.

3. Einige Worte an die Bartender zu besonderer Beachtung.

Dem Herausgeber dieses Werkes liegt es am
Herzen, über einen Punkt, der bisher sehr stark vernachlässigt worden, einige Bemerkungen zu machen.
Wenn man nämlich die verschiedensten Saloons
besucht; sie mögen sehr einfach oder noch so fein
eingerichtet und ausgestattet sein, so wird man
mit wenigen Ausnahmen die Bank (bench), un-
praktisch und schlecht hergerichtet finden. In
dieser Hinsicht möchte ich nun Jedem der einen

8

Saloon oder Barroom zu eröffnen gedenkt, warm
empfehlen dass er diesem Punkte persönliche Aufmerksamkeit schenkt und die Herrichtung der
Bench nicht gänzlich dem Möbeltischler überlässt;
er hat darauf zu achten, dass die Bench bequem
und praktisch hergerichtet wird, dass sie ihrem
Zweck entspricht und jederzeit händig ist, besonders
in Bezug auf die Eis- und Wasser-Behälter, etc.
Auch muss sie genügend lang, breit und bequem
sein, dass man gut Flaschen zwischen dieselbe und
den Counter stellen kann. (Siehe Illustration, No. 2.)
Ferner muss man den Zuckerbehälter so geschickt
placiren, dass man ihn stets bei der Hand hat und
mit dem Suchen keine Zeit verliert. Ein weiterer
wichtiger Punkt ist, die Behälter, welche das Wasser enthalten, stets vollkommen rein zu halten, und
ebenso für die Reinhaltung des Fussbodens zu
sorgen, so dass, wenn einmal ein Kunde hinter die
Bar geht oder blickt, er einen guten Eindruck ge-
winnt. Es muss der Stolz eines jeden Bartenders
sein, sämmtliche Gegenstände, die unter seiner Con-
trolle stehen, in stets gutem und sauberen Zustande
zu halten, so dass er sich nicht zu geniren braucht,
sie jederzeit seinem Principal, sowie irgend einem
Gaste zu zeigen. Je mehr er diese Regeln beobachtet, desto behaglicher wird er sich fühlen und damit
zur Erhaltung seiner Gesundheit viel beitragen.

4. Art und Weise, die Gäste richtig zu behandeln und dabei sich den nöthigen Respect zu verschaffen.

Als allgemeine Regel gilt es in unserem Geschäft,
dass jeder Besitzer oder Bartender seine Gäste mit
Respect , wie ihn die echte Höflichkeit verlangt,
bediene. Ferner ist es von höchster Wichtigkeit,
seinen Gästen stets nur die besten Liqueure, Weine,
Biere, Cigarren, etc., vorzusetzen. Was die Preise
anbelangt, so hat sich jeder nach der Classe seiner
Kundschaft zu richten. Und indem man an seinen

Principien festhält und dem Publikum zeigt, dass
man reell in jeder Beziehung ist, wird man sich die
Achtung Aller und ein gutes Renommee erwerben.
Man thue stets das Rechte, verkaufe niemals Getränke an betrunkene oder unmündige Personen,
oder an Leute, die sich ungebührlich betragen.
Auch sollte man in unserem Geschäft Kunden gegen-
über, mögen sie elegant oder einfach gekleidet sein,
niemals irgend welchen Unterschied machen, so
lange sie sich nur anständig benehmen. Den reichen
Bankier wie den Arbeiter behandele man in derselben
Weise, und verabreiche stets allen Kunden dieselbe
Waare, es müsste denn sein, dass man es mit Leuten
zu thun hätte, die nur auf die Quantität nicht auf
die Qualität Werth legen.

Bei einer derartigen Führung des Geschäfts, indem man es genau so wie jedes andere respectable
Geschäft behandelt, wird man sich rasch und sicher
eine gute Existenz gründen. Schlägt man aber
einen falschen Weg ein, betreibt man das Geschäft
nicht reell, so kann ein Misserfolg nicht ausbleiben.
Auf einen Fehler, den namentlich Viele, die ein
neues Geschäft eröffnen, zu begehen pflegen, möchte
ich noch die Aufmerksamkeit lenken, ich meine
nämlich die Unsitte, übermässig zu tractiren und
Kunden mehr zu geben als sie verlangen und ihnen
zukommt. Auf Ehrenhaftigkeit, Geschick und
tactvolles Benehmen beruhen die Geheimnisse des
Erfolges.

5. Regel für Bartender bei Antritt und Ver-lassen der Bar.

Nachstehende Instructionen beziehen sich auf den
Fall, dass wie es in allen grösseren, feinen Geschäften
üblich ist, die Bartender sich ablösen. Die Bartender welche abgelöst werden haben unbedingt vor
Verlassen der Bar dafür zu sorgen, dass alle Gefässe
und Flaschen für den Gebrauch gefüllt sind, dass
zerschlagenes Eis wie zerschnittene Früchte in ge-

nügender Quantität vorhanden, und dass Bar und
Bench vollständig in Ordnung sind und von den
betreffenden Mixturen nichts fehlt, kurz, dass alles
für den Nachfolger in Bereitschaft liegt, damit derselbe bei Ausübung seines Geschäftes keiner Störung
ausgesetzt ist. Die antretenden Bartender dürfen
sich jedoch nicht unbedingt darauf verlassen dass
Alles in bester Ordnung ist, sondern haben die
Pflicht, die Sachen zu untersuchen, um sich davon
zu überzeugen.

Für die Geschäfte, wo das Checksystem nicht eingeführt ist, sei erwähnt, dass auch die Regulirung
der Casse beim Ablösen vorgenommen werden muss
damit keine Differenzen entstehen. In der Führung
der Casse die für gewöhnlich der Eigenthümer unter
sich hat, liegt eben der Schwerpunkt des Geschäfts.

6. Beschreibung und Verwendung eines Gigger.

In allen nachstehenden Recepten findet sich für
ein gewisses Quantum Flüssigkeit die Bezeichnung
"Weinglas" womit angezeigt wird, dass der Inhalt
eines richtigen Weinglases zur Messung verwendet
werden soll. Das in den Erste-Klasse-Saloons und
Hotels dazu angewandte Mess-Gefäss ist jedoch in
der Regel aus edlem Metall oder von bester Composition, hat die Form eines Sherry-Weinglases, mit
kurzem Stengelfuss, und dieses Gefäss bezeichnet
die englische Sprache mit dem Worte "Gigger."

Jeder Bartender sollte sich beim Mischen von
Getränken eines Giggers bedienen; denn nicht nur
dass beim Gebrauchen desselben die Gäste stets
genau dieselbe Mischung, nicht zu viel und nicht zu
wenig, erhalten und so stets befriedigt werden, sondern es wird auch dadurch der unnützen Verschwen-
dung von Liqueur wirksam vorgebeugt. Nur
Bartender, welche ihr Geschäft gründlich kennen
und langjährige Erfahrung besitzen, könnten ohne
Gebrauch eines Giggers arbeiten, jedoch in jedem
Falle ist die Anwendung desselben vorzuziehen, da

selbst ein Expert namentlich bei starkem Geschäftsgange nicht im Stande ist, die Quantität genau ab-
zumessen.

7. Allgemeine Regeln bei Eröffnung eines neuen Geschäfts.

Die erste Bedingung bei Eröffnung eines neuen
Geschäftes ist die richtige Wahl der Lage; je
glücklicher man darin ist, um so vortheilhafter ist
es für das Geschäft und desto leichter wird es sein
Kunden heranzuziehen. Danach kommt die innere
Austattung, die gesammte Einrichtung, wie sie aus
dem Counter, der vorderen und hinteren Bar, den
Liqueurgefässen, der Toilette und allem sonstigen
Zubehör besteht. Man muss dabei darauf sehen,
die richtige passende Auswahl zu treffen und sich
gänzlich nach der Beschaffenheit des Platzes richten;
das Ganze muss einen angenehmen Eindruck machen,
nicht überladen, aber auch nicht dürftig oder kahl
aussehen. Ein weiterer Punkt, den man nicht ausser Acht lassen darf, ist die Beschaffung der Lease.
Ein jeder, der ein Geschäft anzufangen beabsichtigt,
sei hiermit nachdrücklich gewarnt, dass er sich
rechtzeitig eine Lease auf möglichst viele Jahre
sichere, um nicht den grössten Unannehmlichkeiten
ausgesetzt zu sein. Ferner berechne man sich die
laufenden Ausgaben, wie Rente, Gehälter, Gas, Eis,
Lunch, etc., ganz genau, stelle damit die Einnahmen,
die man zu erwarten hat, zusammen, schätze die
letzteren eher zu niedrig als zu hoch und mache sich
unter Einrechnung des hineingesteckten Capitals
einen sorgfältigen Ueberschlag. Hat man nun alle
Vorbereitungen getroffen, alles genau und einge-
hend erwogen, sich vor allem vor der Unterschreibung
der Lease eine Licenz verschafft, um deren Ertheilung
man nachsuchen muss, und besitzt man das genügende Selbstvertrauen, um das Geschäft in der
gehörigen geschäftsmässigen Weise, ebenso wie
jedes andere zu führen, dann darf man zuversicht-
lich erwarten, in dem Unternehmen erfolgreich zu sein.

8. Erste Pflichten des Bartenders nach Eröffnung des Locales am Morgen.

Das erste, wonach der Bartender zu trachten hat, ist seinem Locale ein möglichst freundliches, einladendes Ansehen zu verleihen und für die Ventilirung desselben je nach der Jahreszeit zu sorgen. Ist dieses geschehen, dann hat der Bartender eine Kanne Eiswasser zurecht zu machen, damit dieses, wenn es verlangt wird, bereits vorhanden ist. Sodann wären sämmtliche Liqueur- und Mixturflaschen aufzufüllen, mit guten Propfen zu versehen, blank zu putzen und wohlgeordnet an ihren Platz zu stellen, sowie Whiskeys, etc., hübsch in den Eisboxen zu placiren, damit diese Getränke stets frisch verabreicht werden können. Ferner hat der Bartender seinen Assistenten anzuweisen, dass derselbe den Boden sowie alle vorhandenen Einrichtungsstücke, letztere mit einem Federwedel sauber reinige, und wenn erforderlich auch Fenster und Spiegel putze. Je blanker der Fussboden und alle Gegenstände gescheuert sind, desto einladender ist der Eindruck, den das Local macht. Nunmehr gehe der Bartender an die Reinigung seiner Bank oder Bench, was auf nachfolgende Art geschieht. Der Bartender nimmt sämmtliche, auf der Bank befindlichen Gläser und Gegenstände und stellt sie inzwischen auf die Bar, wobei er sich jedoch auf einen möglichst kleinen Raum beschränken soll, damit, wenn Gäste kommen, genügend Platz auf der Bar ist, um solche zu bedienen. Ist die Bank frei dann scheure man sie mittelst einer Bürste und Sandseife recht gründlich und wasche sie dann mit reinem Wasser gut ab, damit keine Seifentheile, etc., zurück bleiben, die sich an den Gefässen festhängen könnten. Sodann wasche und putze der Bartender die auf die Bank gehörenden Gläser und Sachen sehr rein und setze sich diese nach seiner besten Bequemlichkeit auf der Bank zurecht, so dass er alles, was er zu seinem

Geschäfte benöthigt, zur Hand hat. Von der
Reinigung der Bank schreite der Bartender zum
Reinigen und Ordnen des rückwärtigen Theiles der
Bar, (back-bar) dessen Gegenstände mehr als Zierde
der Bar dienen, und sehe, dass auch diese durch
Sauberkeit einen freundlichen Eindruck auf den
Gast hervorbringen. Wenn nun in der Zwischen-
zeit der Assistent des Bartenders eine genügende
Quantität Eis für den Tagesgebrauch zerschlagen
hat, dann ziehe der Bartender seine Dienstkleidung
sorgfältig an, damit auch seine Person sich dem
Besucher gefällig präsentire, und zerschneide die für
den Tag nöthigen Früchte, wie Orangen, Citronen,
Ananas, Beeren, Cocktail peels, etc., so, dass sowohl
diese wie seine Bar, Getränke, etc., vollständig in
Ordnung sind, wenn er deren für die Gäste bedarf.
Ferner hat er noch die Pflicht die Wäsche, wie Servietten, Handtücher, welche in genügender Anzahl
vor der Bar zum Gebrauch der Gäste angebracht
sein sollen, zu revidiren und gegen reine zu wech-
seln, wobei noch zu bemerken ist, dass dieses so oft
als nothwendig zu geschehen hat.

Im Uebrigen hat der Bartender besonders darauf
zu achten, dass er seine Morgenarbeit rasch beendige,
damit er sobald als möglich sich in dem sauberen
Costüm zeige, denn nichts ist geeigneter die Gäste
zu vertreiben als der Anblick eines nicht adrett
aussehenden Bartenders. Schliesslich möchte ich
auf eine Unsitte aufmerksam machen, die ich leider
sehr oft zu beobachten Gelegenheit hatte. Nur zu
häufig nämlich vergessen Bartender die vorgesetzten
und schon gebrauchten Gläser Eiswasser wieder
aufzufüllen und so kommt es denn oft vor, dass sich
am Glase kleine Merkmale wiederholten Gebrauches
zeigen und so das Aussehen desselben unappetitlich
machen. Das richtigste ist dem Gaste ein leeres
Glas zugleich mit einer gefüllten Wasserkanne vorzusetzen, damit er sich nach Belieben bedienen
kann.

9. Allgemeine Regel für Oeffnen und Serviren von Champagner.

Wenn eine Gesellschaft Herren Champagner bestellt, hat der Bartender vor Allem die entsprechende
Anzahl Gläser vor die Herren zu stellen und den
Auftraggeber nach der Sorte des zu trinkenden
Champagners zu fragen, sodann muss er sehen, dass
letzterer vom Eis kommt, damit derselbe kalt ist und
gleichzeitig ein Glas oder eine Schüssel mit klein
zerschlagenem Eis nebst Löffeln so stellen, dass sich
die Herren desselben bedienen können. Wenn nun
die Flasche Champagner geöffnet wird, muss zuerst
der Draht entfernt werden, wozu man sich gewöhnlich der Eispicke bedient; sodann zerschneide man
den Bindfaden, wobei nicht ausser Acht gelassen
werden darf, dass dies unter dem Kranze des
Flaschenhalses geschieht, damit der Bindfaden
vollständig abgenommen werden kann. Geschieht
das Zerschneiden des Bindfadens oberhalb des
Flaschenhalses, dann bleiben die unteren Theile
desselben an der Flasche und da an dem Bindfaden stets mehr oder weniger Theile von dem
Verschlusse der Flasche, sei es nun Lack oder
Harz und dergleichen, kleben bleiben, die sich beim
Vollschenken der Gläser loslösen, so fallen solche in
das Glas des Gastes, was selbstverständlich vermieden werden muss. Ist die Flasche soweit geöffnet, dann entferne man den Propfen mittelst
einer Serviette und reinige den Flaschenhals von
etwa daranhängenden Vorschlusstheilen sorgfältig,
worauf das Füllen der Gläser unmittelbar zu folgen
hat. Beim Einschenken von Flaschenweinen überhaupt verlangt die Etiquette, dass der Besteller des
Weines zuerst und zwar nur mit soviel Wein bedient wird damit etwa vom Propfen herrührende
Theile nicht in die Gläser der von ihm eingeladenen
Gäste kommen, und wenn dann alle anderen Gläser
gefüllt sind, wird das Glas des Bestellers vollends
aufgefüllt. Nach dem Füllen der Gläser muss die

FANCY BRANDY SOUR.

Flasche sofort wieder in Eis gestellt werden. Beim Serviren von Champagner an Tischen ist bezüglich des Einschenkens die gleiche Etiquette einzuhalten, ferner darf der Propfen nicht eher entfernt werden, als der Moment des Einschenkens gekommen ist, schliesslich muss in die nächste Nähe des Tisches ein Champagner Cooler gestellt werden, um den Champagner stets kalt zu halten. Will man gefrorenen Wein herstellen, wie er an vielen Plätzen verlangt wird, so nehme man die Weinflasche, stelle sie in den Eis Cooler, fülle diesen mit zerschlagenen Eis und Rock Salz bis zum Rande auf, dann nehme man die Flasche zwischen die' Hände und drehe so lange hin und her, bis eine dicke Masse sich zu bilden anfängt; darauf schneide man den Bindfaden entzwei, ziehe den Cork aus der Flasche, placire darüber eine feine Serviette und fahre mit dem Drehen so lange fort bis der Wein vollständig steif ist. Den auf diese Weise hergestellten Wein nennt man Champagne Frappé.

10. Einige Worte über Lagerbier.

Das Lagerbier, welches ursprünglich ein deutsches Nationalgetränk ist, hat sich namentlich in den verflossenen Jahrzehnten zum Lieblingsgetränk fast aller Nationen emporgeschwungen und erfreut sich besonders in America einer grossen Popularität. Es soll daher auch ganz besonders eines jeden Bartenders Pflicht sein, der Behandlung dieses Getränkes die vollste Aufmerksamkeit zu schenken, da es gerade so viel Beachtung und Accuratesse braucht, wie die meisten anderen Getränke. Die Güte des Biers hängt sehr viel von der richtigen Behandlung ab. Das Lagerbier soll immer frisch, klar und angenehm schmeckend dem Gast verabreicht werden, und muss daher vor dem Verzapfen drei bis vier Tage im Eiskeller oder der Eisbox ruhen können. Die Temperatur des Bieres richtet sich ganz und gar nach der jeweiligen Jahreszeit und darf dasselbe im Sommer nicht warm, im Winter dagegen etwas überschlagen verabreicht werden. Zu kaltes Bier verliert seinen Glanz und Wohlgeschmack. Das wichtigste Erforderniss um stets gutes Bier zu haben, ist eine der Grösse des Umsatzes entsprechende Eisbox oder ein Eiskeller; dieselben müssen im Sommer stets aufgefüllt sein und in gutem Zustande erhalten werden. Wer diese Regeln beobachtet, kann sicher sein, stets gutes Bier zu führen.

11. Regeln beim Verzapfen von Lagerbier.

Die beste und für den Wohlgeschmack des Bieres vortheilhafteste Art des Verzapfens, ist direct vom Fass, indem man den Krahn in das Zapfloch eintreibt, d. h ein Fass ansticht; das Fass dann auf den Bierbock bringt und soviel weglaufen lässt bis klares, helles Bier aus dem Krahnen läuft. Nach den ersten Gläsern muss man am Spund ein Luftventil einschlagen. Wird das Bier durch Röhren geleitet und verzapft, dann ist die Hauptsache, dass die Röhrenleitung aus dem besten Material angefertigt und stets rein gehalten wird. Um bei Röhrenverzapfung dem Bier seine Frische und gutes Aussehen zu bewahren, ist ein entsprechender Luft- oder Wasserdruck unbedingt nothwendig. Wo ein Luftdruckapparat verwendet wird, muss darauf gesehen werden, dass der Luftkessel an einem guten Ort steht. Lässt sich dieses nicht bewerkstelligen, dann ist unbedingt geboten dass dem Luftkessel mittelst einer separaten Röhrenleitung gute reine Luft zugeführt wird Da die Keller, besonders in New York meistens sehr mangelhaft ventilirt sind und feuchte und modrige Luft enthalten, würde sich diese dem ⁿiere mittheilen, und demselben einen schalen und schlechten Geschmack geben, und können auch durch den Genuss solcher Getränke Krankheiten veranlasst werden. Eine weitere Hauptsache ist die öftere Reinigung des Luftkessels, welche wie bei der Röhrenleitung dadurch bewerkstelligt wird,

dass man lauwarmes Wasser, in welchem Waschsoda
aufgelöst wurde, in den Kessel giesst, eine Weile
darin hält und dann durch Oeffnen des unteren
Hahns ablaufen lässt. Nachdem das sodahaltige
Wasser abgelaufen ist giesst man etwas Spiritus in
den Kessel um ihn vollständig zu reinigen. Bier
welches über Nacht in den Röhren gestanden muss
fortgeschüttet und darf nicht verabreicht werden.
Von grosser Wichtigkeit ist das Reguliren des Luft-
oder Wasserdruck-Apparates, und muss jeder Bartender hierin gewissenhaft seine Pflicht erfüllen.
Bei Luftdruckapparaten ist ein regulärer Druck
desshalb von Bedeutung, weil der Bartender bei zu
starkem Druck kein flüssiges Bier sondern lauter
Schaum erhielte, während bei zu schwachem Druck
dass Bier im Fasse matt und schlecht werden würde.
Bei Wasserdruck-Apparaten ist darauf zu sehen,
dass der stärkere Druck, welcher durch den Minder-
verbrauch während des Tages entsteht, regulirt
wird; ferner ist zu empfehlen den Apparat nach
Schliessung des Lokals ganz abzustellen, indem bei
zu grosser Kraftentwickelung ein Platzen der Röhren oder des Fasses zu befürchten wäre. Der Bartender kann deshalb in diesem Punkte nicht zu vorsichtig sein und er sollte so oft als thunlich die
Regulirung überwachen. Die Behandlung des
Flaschenbieres besteht darin, dass es an einem kalten
Ort, aber nicht direct auf Eis aufbewahrt wird. Die
Flaschen sollten stehen, damit die absetzenden
Theile im Bier zu Boden sinken.

Vor allem muss der Bartender darauf achten, dass
die Gläser vollständig rein sind, und dann, wenn er
sie gefüllt hat, streiche er mit einem kleinen Lineal
über den Rand um die Luftblasen zu entfernen, die
sonst den Schaum vernichten und das Bier schaal
machen. Auch möge der Bartender nicht ausser
Acht lassen, wenn er einem Gaste das zweite Glas
Bier einschenkt, stets dasselbe Glas zu gebrauchen,
weil das Bier dann besser schmeckt und aussieht

und den Gast besser zufriedenstellt. Ebenso verfährt man, wenn mehrere Gäste zugleich sich Bier
einschenken lassen, und nimmt bei der zweiten
Runde stets ein Glas nach dem andern zum Auf-
füllen, nicht aber alle auf einmal in die Hand, wie
ich es häufig beobachtet habe, da es unappetitlich
wäre wenn die Gläser verwechselt würden und nicht
jeder das vorher von ihm benutzte Glas erhielte.
Bei starkem Andrange stelle man die gebrauchten
Gläser so auf die Seite, dass jeder Gast sehen kann,
dass er ein frishes Glass erhält. Dies gilt auch für
die Bedienung von Gästen die an Tischen sitzen.
Schliesslich kann ich nicht dringend genug empfehlen, dafür zu sorgen, dass das Bier im Sommer den
richtigen Kältegrad hat, für die heissen Tage 40—45
Grad—und dass es auch im Winter die richtige
Temperatur hat, denn die Gäste legen darauf einen
grossen Werth und pflegen sich Locale in denen das
Bier stets richtig gehalten wird, sehr genau zu
merken.

12. Ueber Behandlung von Flaschenbier.

Die Behandlung des Bieres in Flaschen ist ver-
schieden. Flaschenbier darf niemals direct auf Eis
gelegt werden sondern muss an einem kalten Platz
in der Eisbox aufrecht stehen, so dass der Satz auf
den Boden fällt. Beim Auschenken muss der Bartender darauf sehen, dass er ein sauberes und passen-
des Glas verwendet. Dies ist sowohl bei einheimi-
schen wie importirten Bieren zu beachten.

13. Wie Ale- und Bierröhren zu reinigen.

Wenn der Bartender bemerkt, dass es an der Zeit
ist, die Röhrenleitung zu reinigen, nimmt er dieses
auf folgende Art und Weise am raschesten und
leichtesten vor: Wenn das Bier- oder Ale-Fass leer
ist, nimmt man ein paar Eimer lauwarmes Wasser,
und löst hierin etwa ein Pfund Waschsoda auf, dann
entfernt man das Luftventil am Spund und giesst
das Wasser ins Fass, bringt das Ventil wieder an

und lässt das Wasser etwa eine Stunde darin, dann
dreht man den Apparat an und das sodahaltige
Wasser wird wie das Bier durch die Röhren wieder
herausgetrieben. Ist dies geschehen, so giesst man
noch einige Eimer reines Wasser nach und lässt
dieses wieder durch die Röhren abfliessen.

14. Wie man einen Barroom nebst Toilette in perfectem Zustande erhält.

Es ist die Pflicht eines jeden Bartenders auf pein-
liche Sauberkeit und Accuratesse zu sehen in allem
was mit dem Locale zusammenhängt. Je einladender und gut gehalten die Räumlichkeiten sind, desto
mehr fühlt sich der Gast angezogen und zu längerem
Verweilen aufgelegt. Zudem trägt Reinlichkeit
sehr viel zur Erhaltung der Einrichtung bei. Die
Möbel sollten von Zeit zu Zeit mit gutem Leinöl
abgerieben und polirt werden, wobei man das Holz
vor dem Einölen gut reinigt. Sehr häufig habe ich
die Bemerkung gemacht, dass in manchen Geschäften einzelnen Punkten grosse Aufmerksamkeit ge-
schenkt wird, während andere, wie z. B. die Toilette,
gänzlich vernachlässigt werden. Diese letztere stets
in sauberem und guten Zustand zu erhalten ist eine
der wichtigsten Aufgaben des Besitzers eines Barrooms, indem sehr viele Leute nach dem Aussehen
desselben das ganze Geschäft beurtheilen. Im Winter muss die Toilette gut geheizt sein um gleichzeitig
das sehr lästige und viele Kosten verursachende
Einfrieren der Röhren zu vermeiden. Ausserdem
sollte die Toilette hell und gut ventilirt sein, damit
die Luft darin zu jeder Zeit rein ist. Auch sorge
man ausreichend für feines Toiletten-Papier, sowie
für bequeme Waschgelegenheit, für reine Handtücher, für das Vorhandensein von Bürste und
Kamm, Spucknäpfe, u. s. w. Ich bemerke noch
zum Schluss, dass man die Wichtigkeit dieser Dinge,
die manchem unwesentlich vorkommen mögen, nicht
unterschätzen darf.

15. Behandlung von Liqueuren in Fässern und Flaschen.

Diese Art Getränke, wenn in Fässern, werden in einem Keller oder Magazin bei mässiger Temperatur aufbewahrt, indem man die Fässer in wagrechter Lage mit dem Spund nach oben auf einem Lager, sog. "Skid," placirt, damit sie vor der Feuchtigkeit des Bodens geschützt sind. Sollte die Abzapfung mittelst eines Hahnes geschehen, dann ist solcher vor dem Auflegen des Fasses auf dem " Skid" einzutreiben. Flaschenliquöre müssen ebenfalls bei mässiger Temperatur in wagrechter Lage aufbewahrt werden, damit der Pfropfen stets feucht bleibt und nicht eintrocknen kann, da sonst der Liqueur an Stärke und Wohlgeschmack verliert.

16. Wie man den Geschmack des Gastes ausfindig macht.

Die grösste Genugthuung findet der Gast darin, wenn der Bartender es versteht, das von ihm gewünschte Getränk, im Falle es ein gemischtes Getränk ist, in zusagender Weise zu bereiten. Der Bartender muss sich erkundigen ob das Getränk stark oder schwach, mehr oder weniger süss oder sauer geliebt wird, um die Mischung dem Geschmacke des Gastes entsprechend zu machen. Die in diesem Buche vom Herausgeber zusammengestellten Recepte sind absolut vorschriftsmässig und dem Geschmack der Mehrheit des Publikums angepasst; es ist jedoch manches Mal nöthig, eben je nach dem eigenthümlichen Geschmacke des einen oder andern Gastes die Mischung vorzunehmen. Der Bartender muss seine ganze Aufmerksamkeit dem Studium des Geschmackes der in seinem Locale verkehrenden Gäste widmen, und wird derselbe, je mehr er sich in dieser Beziehung zu vervollkommnen versteht, bei den Gästen in Achtung stehen und beliebt sein.

17. Wie eine Punchbowle zu eisen oder abzukühlen ist.

Zur Eisung oder Abkühlung einer Punchbowle bedient man sich eines grösseren und umfangreicheren Gefässes als die Bowle selbst, in der Regel einer Blechschüssel. In die Blechschüssel stelle man nun die Bowle und fülle den Zwischenraum zwischen derselben und der Schüssel mit fein zerschlagenem Eis und zwar so, dass selbst über dem Rand der Bowle das Eis noch einen Kranz bildet. Um das Eis compact zu machen, gebe man hin und wieder eine leichte Schicht Rocksalz bei. Sodann garnire man den Eiskranz in zierlicher Weise mit kleinen Blättern und Saisonfrüchten, wie Erdbeeren, etc., und versehe auch das Aeussere der Blechschüssel mit einer Servietten-Draperie, so dass die Bowle einen hübschen Eindruck macht. Der Bartender muss sodann darauf achten, für das geschmolzene Eis Ersatz nachzufüllen und immer etwas Salz dazwischen zu streuen. Vortheilhaft ist es ferner, wenn die Blechschüssel unterhalb mit einem kleinen Hahn versehen ist, um das Wasser ablassen zu können.

18. Serviren von Getränken an Tischen.

Wenn eine Herrengesellschaft irgendwelche Liqueure bestellt, so hat der Bartender die nöthige Anzahl Gläser mit den betreffenden Getränken in den Flaschen an den Tisch zu bringen oder zu schicken, damit sich die Gäste selbst nach Wunsch bedienen können. Auch muss für jeden der Gäste eine Serviette beigelegt werden. Im Falle in dem betreffenden Lokale ein Markensystem eingeführt ist, so überreiche man die entsprechende Marke sogleich bei Verabreichung des Getränkes an den Besteller in bescheidener Art. Da dies ein allgemeiner Gebrauch ist, wird es nie Anstoss erregen, und dient gleichzeitig zur Verhütung von Confu-

sionen. Die Gläser lässt man so lange auf dem
Tische stehen, bis sich die Gesellschaft entfernt
hat.

19. Behandlung französsischer Rothweine, etc.

Diese Weine müssen sehr sorgfältig behandelt
werden, da dieselben durchgehends mehr oder
weniger einen Niederschlag (Satz) bilden, welcher,
wenn aufgerüttelt, den Wein trübe machen würde.
Es ist daher beim Aufnehmen der Flaschen und
Einschenken die grösste Behutsamkeit nöthig. Um
die Flaschen nicht unmittelbar aus einer wagrechten
Stellung in eine stehende bringen zu müssen, wodurch ein Aufschütteln fast unvermeidlich ist, bedient man sich zur Aufbewahrung eines sogenannten Weinschiffes oder Weinkorbes, worin die Flaschen in schräger Stellung liegen. Die Temperatur
welche bei diesen Weinen beobachtet werden muss,
variirt zwischen 60 und 70° Fahrenheit.

20. Praktische Winke über das Einkaufen der verschiedenen Getränke im Grossen.

Ein Jeder mache es sich zur Regel, nur mit ersten,
durchaus respectablen Firmen in Geschäftsverbind-
ung zu treten und von solchen nur Waaren und
Getränke im Grossen zu kaufen. Verfährt man so,
dann kann man sicher sein stets gute und preis-
werthe Waare zu erhalten. Man begnüge sich mit
bescheidenem Gewinn, was sich auf die Dauer als
sehr vortheilhaft erweisen wird, denn nicht nur dass
man sich dadurch ein gutes Rennommé schafft, auch
dass Vertrauen der Gäste wird man auf diese Art
gewinnen.

21. Behandlung von Ale und Porter in Fässern.

Sämmtliche Fässer mit Ale oder Porter müssen
angezapft werden, ehe sie auf die betreffende Stellage
den sogenannten "Skid" gelegt werden, und ist dabei
zu beachten, dass sie unterlegt sind, damit sie nicht
aus ihre Lage gebracht werden, da in Ale und Porter

PLATE No. 12.

MISSISSIPPI PUNCH.   CURAÇOA PUNCH.

die Gährungsstoffe noch enthalten sind. Aus demselben Grunde müssen die Fässer vor dem Abzapfen hinreichende Ruhe gehabt haben, damit sie die Gährungsstoffe auf den Boden niederschlagen können und das Getränk klar ist. Die Temperatur darf nicht zu kalt und nicht zu warm sein, wenn das Getränk gut munden soll. Ferner muss man darauf achten, dass man die verschiedenen Sorten Ale genügende Zeit auf Lager hat, ehe man sie ausschenkt; Z. B. Bass Ale, verlangt von 1 bis 6 Wochen Ruhe, ehe es ganz hell ist. Altes Ale verlangt auch eine geraume Zeit, ehe man es ausschenken kann. Neues Ale gebraucht in der Regel nur kurze Zeit, um vollständig klar zu werden. Jedoch je länger man sämmtliche Ale-Sorten auf Lager hält, um so mehr werden sie sich entwickeln, und an Geschmack gewinnen. Ferner darf man unter keinen Umständen vergessen, sämmtliche Ales und Porter anzuzapfen, bevor sie auf den Skid gelegt werden, damit sie in ihrer Lage ungestört liegen bleiben.

22. Regeln bei Verzapfung von Ale und Porter.

Die Verzapfung von Ale und Porter geschieht am Besten direct vom Fasse, d. h. im Locale selbst, mittelst eines Hahnes oder. Krahnens. Wenn jedoch der Raum die Lagerung eines Fasses nicht zulässt, und die Verzapfung vom Keller aus mittelst Röhren geschehen muss, ist unbedingt darauf zu sehen, dass die Röhren nur vom besten Material angefertigt sind. Das Ale welches über Nacht in den Röhren gestanden, darf niemals einem Gaste gereicht werden, sondern man muss so viel ablaufen lassen, bis ein vollständig reines und klares Getränk erlangt wird. Bei Verzapfung durch Röhrenleitung muss jeder Bartender auf die allersorgfältigste Reinigung der Röhren bedacht sein. Das Getränk muss bei einer mässigen Temperatur gehalten werden, da es durch Kälte trüb wird. Ale in Flaschen wird

liegend aufbewahrt, nur die für den nächsten Ge-
brauch bestimmten Flaschen lasse man an kühler
Stelle 3 bis 4 Tage stehen, damit der Satz auf dem
Boden sich sammle. Beim Hantiren muss man vorsichtig sein, damit der Satz nicht aufgerührt wird
und sich mit der Flüssigkeit vermischt. Was die
Temperatur des hinter der Bar verzapften Ale und
Porter anbetrifft, so richte man sich ganz nach dem
Wetter; ist es kalt so ist Eis unnöthig, bei warmem
Wetter aber lege man Eis auf die Röhren. Schenkt
man Ale aus einer Flasche ein, so muss der Bartender beim Herausziehen des Corks die Flasche
nicht schütteln. Wenn man eine Flasche Bass oder
Scotch Ale für einen Gast allein einschenkt, so
nehme man ein genügend grosses Glas, welches den
ganzen Inhalt der Flasche fasst, denn bei zweima-
ligem Einschenken wird man das Ale nicht so klar
erhalten als es sein sollte. Wenn man Ale gleichzeitig für zwei oder drei Gäste einschenkt, so halte
man die Gläser in der linken Hand und giesse dass
Ale durch langsames Umkippen der Flasche ein,
damit die Flüssigkeit recht klar und schön heraus-
kommt und die Gäste befriedigt werden.

23. Behandlung von Mineralwasser.

Die Mineralwasser sollen an einem kalten Ort
aufbewahrt werden, damit man sie ohne Zusatz von
Eis trinken kann. Stark moussirende Mineralwasser
wie Syphon Selters, u. s. w., müssen successive einer
kalten Temperatur ausgesetzt werden, da durch zu
plötzliche Abkühlung, leicht eine Explosion veranlasst wird, indem sich die darin enthaltenen Gase
entwickeln. Derartige Explosionen hatten schon
sehr verderbliche Folgen. Die Temperatur der
Mineralwasser ist in der Regel von 35 bis 50 Grad.

24. Garniren gemischter Getränke.

Beim Garniren gemischter Getränke muss der
Bartender sich merken, dass die zur Garnitur bestimmten Früchte bei nicht geseihten Getränken

nach erfolgter Mischung mit einer zierlichen Gabel
auf dem Getränke geschmackvoll vertheilt werden
müssen. Bei geseihten Getränken werden die betreffenden Früchte mittelst einer Gabel in das leere
Glas placirt und dann das Getränk darauf geseiht.
(Siehe Illustration.)

25. Regel in Betreff des Lunch.

Es ist jetzt allgemein gebräuchlich den Gästen
Lunch zur Verfügung zu stellen. Dabei hat man
in erster Linie darauf zu achten, dass Alles was man
vorsetzt nicht nur geniessbar ist, sondern auch recht
sauber servirt wird. Der Fussboden in der Nähe
des Lunchcounter muss von Abfällen rein gehalten
werden. Wenn man diese Punkte vernachlässigt
wird der Lunch anstatt den Appetit anzuregen, bei
vielen Gästen das Gegentheil bewirken.

26. Behandlung von Früchten, Milch und Eiern.

Früchte, Milch und Eier müssen an einem kalten
Ort aufbewahrt werden, um sie länger vor Verderben und Fäulniss zu schützen. Da die Fäulniss bei
Obst schnell um sich greift, sollte besonders Tafel-
obst täglich nachgesehen und die angefaulten entfernt werden. Zerschnittene Früchte die vom vor-
hergehenden Tag übrig blieben sollten nicht zu gemischten Getränken verwendet werden, da sie ihr
Aroma verloren haben und den Geschmack des Getränks verderben. Frische Milch sollte nicht zu der
schon vorräthigen geschüttet werden um Sauerwer-
den zu verhindern. Milchbehälter müssen täglich
gereinigt und geschlossen gehalten werden.

27. Oeffnen von Flaschen mit Metallcapseln.

Wenn die zu öffnende Flasche mit einer Metall-
capsel versehen ist, schneide man mit einem Messer
den Deckel der Capsel oberhalb des Flaschenhalses
ab, entcorke die Flasche und reinige mittelst einer
Serviette die Flaschenöffnung. Der untere Theil
der Capsel an dem Halse der Flasche gibt dieser ein
hübscheres Aussehen.

28. Wie Champagner und andere Weine zu behandeln.

Beim Oeffnen und Auspacken der Kisten oder Körbe, sowie bei der Einlagerung von Champagner ist grosse Vorsicht nöthig, da im Champagner bekanntlich so viel Kohlensäure enthalten ist, dass selbst ein geringer Stoss eine Explosion der Flasche veranlassen kann. Bei Champagner, wie überhaupt bei allen Arten von Weinen in Flaschen, gilt hinsichtlich der Aufbewahrung die gleiche Vorschrift einer wagerechten Lage, damit der Pfropfen feucht bleibt und nicht eintrocknen kann, da sonst der Wein an Stärke und Blume verliert. Wenn mehr Champagner auf Eis gelegt wurde als Verwendung fand sollte er auf dem Eise verbleiben bis er verlangt wird. Da öfterer Temperaturwechsel dem Champagner schadet.

29. Wie man Silber-Geschirr, Spiegel, etc., putzt.

Man wird das Putzen von Silbergeschirr, etc., sehr leicht bewerkstelligen wenn man wie folgt verfährt: Als Putzpulver nehme man No. 2 Whitening, und löse dasselbe in Wasser oder Spiritus auf, dass es dünnflüssig bleibt. Bevor man die Lösung aufträgt müssen die zu putzenden Gegenstände gut abgewaschen und von allem daran haftenden Schmutz befreit werden, dann trage man die Lösung auf und lasse sie antrocknen. Wenn dies erfolgt ist reibe man den Gegenstand mit einem reinen Tuche oder Chamoisleder tüchtig ab, worauf er vollständig blank polirt sein wird. Bei Vertiefungen wo man mit dem Tuche nicht ankommen kann bediene man sich einer Silberbürste. Zum Putzen der Spiegel gebrauche man ein reines, feuchtes Handtuch um sämmtliche Flecke zu entfernen, dann nehme man ein reines trockenes Handtuch oder Chamoisleder, und reibe mit diesem bis das Glas rein und blank ist. Man

nehme nur leinene Handtücher, wie sie zum Putzen
von Gläsern benutzt werden.

30. Liqueure, Bitters und Syrup.

Diese müssen in einem Raum bei mässiger Temperatur aufbewahrt werden, und ist durch guten
Verschluss vermittelst Pfropfen u. dergl. das Ein-
dringen von Insecten unmöglich zu machen.

31. Form der Gläser für durchgeseihte Getränke.

Der Bartender muss bei Bereitung zu seihender
Getränke beachten, dass er sich eines schönen, appe-
titlichen Glases bedient; das Glas darf keinesfalls
zu klein sein, um die ganze durchgeseihte Masse
fassen zu können, soll aber auch nicht unverhältniss-
mässig gross sein. In der Wahl des Glases liegt
viel, dem Gaste das betreffende Getränk einladend
zu machen.

32. Verabreichung von Bar Löffel bei gemischten Getränken.

Der Bartender darf nicht unterlassen, jedem gemischten Getränk einen Barlöffel beizugeben, und
zwar bedient man sich bei Getränken in kleinen
Gläsern, wie man sie zu Whiskey, Gin Toddy, etc.,
benutzt, der kurzen Barlöffel, während bei Getränken
in grösseren Gläsern, Limonade, Punsch, etc., die
Löffel mit langen, gewundenen Stielen benutzt werden. Viele der Gäste pflegen das Getränk erst zu
versuchen, um wenn zu stark, Wasser nachzufüllen.
Andere wollen gewisse Fruchtstücke aus den gemischten Getränken herausholen, etc., und zu allen
diesen Hantirungen bedürfen sie eines Löffels, der
daher mit servirt werden muss. Hübsche, zierliche
Barlöffel sind sehr zu empfehlen.

33. Einige Worte über die Eisbox.

Eine grosse Nothwendigkeit ist es die Eisbox in
gutem und durchaus sauberen Zustande zu halten.
Die darin aufzubewahrenden Gegenstände, stelle
man an dafür bestimmte Plätze, damit sie stets zur

Hand sind und man keine Zeit mit Suchen verliert.
Auch versäume man nicht die Abzugsröhren rein zu
halten. Man wird sich dadurch viel Aergerniss und
unnütze Arbeit ersparen. Wenn der Eigenthümer
die Eisbox selber bauen lässt, sollte er darauf sehen,
dass dieselbe einen dem Geschäft entsprechenden
Umfang hat, aus dem besten Holze verfertigt und
gut und dauerhaft ausgefüttert wird. Auf diese
Weise erhält man eine leistungsfähige Eisbox.

34. Wie man Keller und Lagerraum zu halten hat.

Beim Halten der Keller wie des Lagerraums ist
sehr zu beachten, dass beide so sauber wie nur irgend
möglich aussehen und gut ventilirt sind, damit die
Luft stets recht frisch und rein sei und nie ein übler
Geruch zu bemerken ist, wie man ihn leider zu häufig
findet. Ich möchte auf das dringendste empfehlen,
diesen Theil des Geschäftsraumes ebenso sauber zu
halten wie die Bar. Mit Flaschen und überhaupt
Allem, was in den Lagerraum gehört, gehe man
sorgfältig um, halte die verschiedenen Sorten von
einander getrennt, so dass Alles seinen bestimmten
Platz hat und zu jeder Zeit ohne Zeitverlust gefun-
den werden kann. Die leeren Flaschen halte man
getrennt für sich und lege sie auf ein Gestell, damit
sie zur Hand sind wenn man sie brauchen will. Der
Boden des Kellers muss stets sauber und trocken
gehalten werden. Im Sommer, wenn das Eishaus
gefüllt wird, muss man nachsehen, dass der Boden
nicht feucht gelassen wird.

35. Wie man das Geld von den Gästen erhält.

Beim Einfordern und Einnehmen des Geldes kann
man nicht vorsichtig genug verfahren, denn darin
liegt naturgemäss der Schwerpunkt des Geschäfts.
Die richtige Art und Weise ist, schon während man
die Gäste bedient den Betrag den man zu fordern
hat genau zusammenzurechnen, damit die Gäste,
wenn sie fragen was sie schuldig sind, nicht lange

auf Antwort zu warten brauchen. Das Kleingeld
welches die Kunden zurückerhalten lege man auf
höfliche Weise direct vor dieselben. Bei sehr starkem Geschäftsgange hat der Bartender besonders
darauf zu achten, dass Niemand das Local verlässt
ohne bezahlt zu haben. Je genauer man alle diese
Regeln befolgt, um so vortheilhafter wird es sich für
das Geschäft erweisen. Einen durchaus ungeschäfts-
mässigen Eindruck macht es, wenn der Bartender,
wie ich es oft beobachtet habe, mit dem Wechselgeld
Spielerei treibt. Ich halte es für den einzig richtigen
Weg, das Wechselgeld auf eine trockene Stelle des
Counters so hinzulegen, dass man einen etwaigen
Irrthum sofort bemerken und corrigiren kann. Zum
Schluss möchte ich noch erwähnen, dass die Gewohn-.
heit vieler Bartender, das Wechselgeld dem Gast in·
die Hand zu geben, falsch und fehlerhaft ist, denn
sollte dabei ein Versehen vorkommen, so kann es
der betreffende Bartender nicht corrigiren.

36. Wie Metall-Gegenstände zu putzen.

Es ist und sollte der Stolz für jeden Besitzer und
Bartender eines öffentlichen Lokales sein, sämmtliche Metall-Gegenstände so blank als möglich zu
haben. Geht man mit den Ale und Liqueur Maassen,
Bier-Drips und mit allem was sonst dazu gehört,
recht sorgfältig um, so wird man ausfinden, dass
dies lange nicht so viel Zeit erfordert als manche
Leute sich einbilden, wenn man jeden Tag die Gegenstände mit Putzpulver gründlich und sauber abreibt.
Diese Arbeit darf in keinem Geschäfte vernach-.
lässigt werden

37. Nothwendigkeit einer genauen Preisliste.

Für jedes Geschäft unserer Branche ist es in erster
Linie nöthig, eine vollständige und übersichtliche
Preisliste zu führen. Dies wird sich für das Geschäft als sehr vortheilhaft erweisen. Zudem wird
dadurch beim Verkauf per Flasche manchen leicht

entstehenden Irrthümern vorgebeugt, namentlich wenn der Bartender noch nicht lange in dem betreffenden Geschäft und mit den gebräuchlichen Preisen noch nicht recht vertraut ist.

38. Ueber Behandlung von Glaswaaren.

Obwohl bereits die Wichtigkeit reiner Gläser besprochen ist, soll dennoch auch an dieser Stelle wiederholt werden, dass es eine Hauptpflicht des Bartenders ist, die im Gebrauche befindlichen Gläser stets mit aller Sorgfalt zu reinigen und zu putzen und niemals unreine oder nasse Gläser, sei es nun zu einfachen oder gemischten Getränken, verwenden. Es muss der Stolz des Bartenders sein, alles was zum Geschäfte gehört in musterhafter Ordnung und Reinlichkeit zu haben. Bemerkt sei noch, dass jeder Bartender zum Reinigen seiner Gläser ein besonderes Handtuch bereit halten muss, welches er in keinem Falle zu anderen Zwecken verwenden darf.

39. Behandlung der Cigarren.

In den Geschäften, welche Cigarren führen, ist es die Pflicht des Bartenders darauf zu sehen, dass die Gäste auch in diesem Punkte zufrieden gestellt werden, und dass man sorgfältig dem Geschmacke jedes Einzelnen Rechnung trage. Im Sommer achte man darauf, dass die Cigarren nicht zu feucht werden und im Winter empfiehlt es sich in den Cigarren-Case einen nassen Schwamm zu legen, da die Atmosphäre in Folge der Heizens sehr trocken zu sein pflegt. Auf diese Weise werden sich die Cigarren am besten halten.

40. Wie Syrups gegen das Eindringen von Insecten zu schützen sind.

Syrups werden, so lange sie sich in Aufbewahrung an einem kühlen Orte befinden, gegen Insecten unbedingt gesichert, wenn der Bartender nicht unterlässt, die betreffenden Gefässe gut zu verkorken, überhaupt gut zu verschliessen. Bei Syrups welche sich bereits in den Mixturflaschen befinden, empfiehlt es sich diese in eine mit Wasser gefüllte Untertasse zu stellen, wodurch dem kriechenden Insect der Zugang zur Flasche abgeschnitten wird. Diese Vorsicht wird auch bei Zucker gut angewendet.

41. Ueber das Verhängen der Bar-Einrichtung während der Sommerzeit.

Während der Sommerzeit war es stets Sitte, die Bareinrichtung und die Gaskronen in netter und geschmackvoller Weise zu verhängen, damit nicht Fliegen und andere Insecten ihre Spuren darauf zurück lassen. Dabei ist aber hauptsächlich zu beachten, dass man vor der Verhängung und Ausschmückung die gesammte Einrichtung einer gründlichen Reinigung unterziehe. Eine hübsche Bekleidung nimmt sich sehr vortheilhaft aus und macht ein Lokal ansprechender.

42. Ueber Hantirung des Eises im Allgemeinen.

Was die für unser Geschäft so wichtige Eisfrage anbelangt, so empfiehlt es sich, eine eigene Waage zu haben, um den Händler zu controlliren. Vor allem achte man darauf, dass das Eis stets vollkommen rein sei und keine Schnee- oder Schmutz-Spuren an sich trage. Das Richtige ist, das Eis, bevor man es in die Box oder den Keller legt, gründlich abzuwaschen. An heissen Tagen ist zu beobachten, dass man die Box stets ganz gefüllt hat. Das Eis ferner, welches man für gemischte Getränke gebraucht, muss man sorgfältig abwaschen, damit es vollständig sauber ist. Zum Schlusse sei noch bemerkt, dass man kleine, zerschlagene Eisstücke, niemals mit den Fingern anfasse, sondern sich stets dazu einer kleinen Eisschaufel bediene, da es sonst einen unappetitlichen Eindruck machen würde.

43. Schlussworte.

Nach all' den Regeln und Winken, die ich in diesem Buch über die Führung, das Benehmen und Aussehen eines Bartenders gegeben, könnte ich es jetzt genug sein lassen, aber es drängt mich am Schlusse angelangt, noch verschiedene Bemerkungen zu wiederholen und die Befolgung derselben jedem einzelnen auf's wärmste und dringendste an's Herz zu legen und zur sorgfältigsten Beachtung zu empfehlen. Es betrifft Kleinigkeiten, die mancher Kurzsichtige vielleicht für gänzlich unbedeutend hält, die aber sehr störend wirken, wenn sie nicht beachtet werden. Zunächst kann der Bartender nicht sauber und adrett genug aussehen, ferner halte man nie, wenn man hinter der Bar steht, Zahnstocher im Munde, mache sich nicht mit der Nase zu schaffen, reinige niemals die Fingernägel, kämme nicht das Haar oder spucke auf den Fussboden, halte keine Cigarre im Munde, und versäume nicht, nach Verlassen der Toilette sieh die Hände zu waschen auch vermeide man, wenn es irgend möglich, hinter der Bar seine Mahlzeiten einzunehmen, kurz all' diese Verrichtungen und theils üblen Angewohnheiten unterlasse man in Gegenwart von anderen Personen. Ueberhaupt thue man nichts, was einen unangenehmen Eindruck auf den Gast macht und geeignet wäre, das Geschäft zu schädigen. Besondere Sorgfalt verwende man auf die Reinhaltung der Hände, die stets sauber, trocken und gut gehalten sein müssen. In keinem Falle glaube einer durch schlechte, unfeine Manieren, wie sie leider so manche selbstgefällig zur Schau tragen, imponiren und einen Eindruck machen zu können. Je feiner, zurückhaltender und tactvoller sich der Bartender benimmt, um so mehr Respect wird er sich verschaffen und seinem Stande um so grössere Ehre einlegen. Das Geheimniss ein vollendeter Bartender zu sein, beruht nicht nur darauf, dass man sein

Geschäft gründlich versteht und betreibt, sondern auch, dass man sich als Gentleman beträgt.

44. Verzeichniss sämmtlicher Utensilien, etc., in einem Saloon.

Indem der Verfasser diese Liste unterbreitet, möchte er bemerken, dass diese Gegenstände complet nicht in jedem Saloon absolut verhanden sein müssen, sondern nur in Geschäften erster Classe. Jedermann, der sich ein solches Geschäft einrichtet, beschafft sich die Gegenstände je nach Bedarf; da es hingegen nöthig ist, die Gegenstände wenigstens zu kennen so wurde die folgende Liste zusammengestellt:

Liqueur Maasse,
Gallone,
Halbe Gallone,
Quart, (zwei pint)
Pint,
Halb-Pint,
Gill, ($^1/_4$ pint)
Halb-Gill,
Liqueur-Pumpe,
Bierschlägel,
Filtrir-Sack oder Papier,
Bier und Ale Hähne,
Bohrer,
Liqueur Messer,
Nagelbohrer,
Bier und Ale Maasse,
Spundschlägel,
Gummischlauch zum Abziehen,
Liqueurlabel,
Thermometer,
Trichter,
Pfropfenzieher,

Kessel für heisses Wasser,
Eiswasserkanne auf die Bar,
Citronenpresse,
Bier und Ale Ventile,
Eispicke,
Eiskübel, (cooler)
Eisschaufel,
Eisstössel,
Liqueur Gigger, (Messgefäss),
Becher zum Schütteln von Getränken,
Barlöffel, (lange und kurze)
Julep oder Punch Seiher,
Gewürzgefässe,
Ale Mugs,
Pfropfenzange,
Glas- oder Scheuerbürste,
Pfropfen, (diverse)
Pfropfenpresse,

Patent Champagnerhahn
Syrupkanne,
Honigkanne,
Fruchtmesser, (lang)
Zuckerlöffel, (gross)
Zuckerzange,
Schneeschläger,
Zuckereimer, (Pail)
Muscatnussbüchse,
Muscatnussreibe,
Bisquitteller oder Bowle,
Zuckerbowle mit Deckel,
Pfefferbüchsen,
Fruchtteller,
Schöpflöffel für Punsch,
etc.,
Federwedel,
Besen,
Silberbürste,
Tom and Jerry Bowle,
Tom and Jerry Cups,
Mop, Stiel und Wringer,
Handtücher,
Servietten,
Spucknäpfe,
Fruchtgabel,
Weinkorb,
Weinschiff,
Cigarrenteller oder Korb,
Liqueur und Wein Eti-
quetten,
Holzeimer oder Pail,
Streichholzbüchsen,
Streichhölzer,
Kamm und Haarbürste,
Toilet Papier,
Putzpulver für Silber,
Schrot,
Einwickelpapier,

Zahnstocher,
Schreibpapier und Cou-
verte,
Bindfaden,
Postkarten,
Briefmarken,
Tinte und Feder,
Gummi arab. (flüssig)
Geschäftskarten,
Kreide,
Adresskalender,
Zeitungen,
Geschäftsbücher,
Waschseife,
Sandseife,
Toiletseife,
Korbflaschen, (gross und
klein)
Mixturflaschen,
Julep Strohhalme,
Fensterbürste,
Stufenleiter,
Präsentirteller,
Oel, (um Bargegenstände
einzureiben)
Tafel Salz-Box,
Rail Road Guide,
Lineal, (Zum Abstrei-
chen des Bierschaum)
Spanisch Rohr,
Liqueurflaschen,
Reise oder Feldflasche
(gross und klein)
Schwamm,
Staubschaufel,
Bieruntersätze,
Segar Bags,
Celery Salz-Box,
City Directory.

45. Verzeichniss der Glaswaaren.

Champagner Goblets,
Champagner Weingläser,
Rheinwein Gläser,
Sherrywein Gläser,
Absinthe Gläser,
Sauer Gläser,
Whiskey Gläser,
Cordial Gläser,
Hot Apple Toddy Gläser,
Pony Bier Gläser,
Tom and Jerry Cups,
Glass Jar for Julep Straws,
Champagner Cocktail Gläser,

Julep oder Cobbler Gläser
John und Tom Collins Gläser,
Claret Wein Gläser,
Portwein Gläser,
Mineralwasser Gläser,
Cocktail Gläser,
Heisswasser Gläser,
Pony Cognac Gläser,
Wasser Gläser,
Ale, Porter und Bier Gläser,
Ale Mugs,
Finger Bowls, (für Barlöffel und Seiher).

Wenn man die betreffenden Gläser kauft, so achte man darauf, dass sie so schön wie möglich sind und zu einander passen.

46. Verzeichniss sämmtlicher Sorten Getränke, Mixturen, etc.

Cognac, (Brandy) (verschiedene Sorten)
Bourbon Whiskey,
Scotch Whiskey,
Old Tom Gin,
St. Croix Rum,
Blackberry Brandy,
Spiritus,

Rye Whiskey,
Irish Whiskey,
Holland Gin,
Jamaica Rum,
Apple Jack or Brandy,
Arrac,
Medford Rum.

47. Weine.

Champagner,
Sauterne Weine,
Rhein und Mosel Weine,
Bordeaux Weine,
Catawba Weine,
Spanische Weine,

Port Weine (roth u. weiss)
Claret Weine, (Franz. Rothweine)
Madeira Weine,
Ungarische Weine, (roth und weiss)

California Weine,
Tokayer Weine,
Sherry Weine,

Burgunder Weine,
und andere Sorten.

48. Cordials.

Dieses ist eine vollständige Liste sämmtlicher französichen Liqueure, die in unserem Geschäft mehr oder weniger gebraucht werden.

Absinthe, (grün und weiss)
Curaçoa, (roth und weiss)
Maraschino Dalmatico,
Creme de Mocca,
Anisette de Martinique,
Eau d'Amour, (Liebes-Wasser)
Vermouth,
Allash Russian Kümmel,
Creme de Nogau,
Vanilla,
Creme d'Ananas,
China—China,
Creme d'Anisette,
Huile de fleurs d'oranges,
Creme de Peppermint,
Amourette,
Eau de Calame, (Calmus Liqueur)
Creme de Muscat,
Creme de Chocolade,
Angelica,
Eau celeste, (Himmels-Wasser)
Boonekamp of Magbitter,
Creme au lait, (Milch-Liqueur)
Liqueur de la Grande Chartreuse, (weiss)

Liqueur de la Grande Chartreuse, (grün)
Benedictine,
Chartreuse, (grün und gelb)
Eau d'or A, (Gold-Wasser)
Parfait d'Amour,
Curaçoa de Marseille,
Kirschwasser,
Anisette,
Danziger Goldwasser,
Boquet de Dames, .
Berlin Gilka,
Eau de belles femmes,
Huile d'Angelica,
Eau de pucelle, (Jungfern Wasser)
Maraschino di Zara,
Curaçoa Imperial,
Creme aux Bergamottes,
Creme de Canelle,
Mint Cordial,
Eau d'argent, (Silber-Wasser)
Creme de Cacao,
Krambambuli,
Creme de Menthe, (Pfefferminz Liqueur)
Creme aux Amanda, (Mandel Creme)

Liqueur de la Grande Chartreuse, (yellow)

Creme de Noisette a la Rose.

49. Ales und Porter.

Bass Ale in Fässer und Flaschen,
Scotch Ales, (Muir & Sons)
Scotch Ales, (Robert Younkers)
New and Old Ales,
Flaschen Bier, (importirt und einheimisch)

Guinness extra Stout, (Fässer und Flaschen importirt)
Stock Ales,
Porter,
Lagerbier,
Flaschen Ales und Porter, (importirt und einheimisch)

50. Mineralwasser, etc.

Belfast Ginger Ale,
Kissinger Wasser,
Congress Wasser,
Vichy Wasser,
Lemon und plain Soda Wasser,
Sarsaparilla,
Carbonic Acid,

Domestic Ginger Ale,
Apollinaris Wasser,
Imp. Selters Wasser,
Syphon Selters Wasser,
Hathorn Wasser,
Cider,
Acid Syphon,

51. Syrups.

White Gum Syrup,
Pineapple (Ananas) Syrup,
Erdbeer Syrup,
Orchard (Frucht) Syrup,

Orgeat Syrup,
Himbeer Syrup,
Citronen Syrup,
Orangen Syrup,
Rock Candy Syrup,

52. Bitters.

Boker's, (genuine only)
Dieses Bitter hat den alten Ruf bewahrt und ist stets noch in starker Nachfrage.

Hostetters Bitters,
Orangen Bitters,
Boonecamp Bitters,
Stoughton Bitters,
Sherry Wein Bitters,

53. Früchte.

Aepfel,	Orangen,
Pfirsiche,	Citronen,
Limes,	Ananas,
Trauben,	Erdbeeren,
Brombeeren,	

54. Mixturen, etc.

Tansy,	Wormwood,
Calmus oder Flag Root,	Eier,
Schwarzer Molasses,	Zucker, (Stück und pul-
Milch,	versirten)
Jamaica Ginger,	Pfefferminz,
Krausemünze, (Mint)	Pfeffer, (roth u. schwarz)
Condensirte Milch,	Calisaya,
Muscatnüsse,	Nelken,
Zimmt,	Gebranntes Korn,
Salz,	Celery Salz,
Pfeffer Sauce,	Beef Extract,
Bicarbonate of Soda,	Celery Syrup.
Honig,	

55. Verschiedenes.

Cigarren,	Tabak,
Cigarretten,	Kautabak.

---

56. Champagne Cocktail.
(Gebraucht ein Champagner Goblet.)

Wenn man Getränke wie Cocktails mischt, ist es eine Regel, dass man das Glas mit klein zerschlagenem Eis füllt, ehe man die entsprechenden Ingredienzen hinein thut, wenn man aber einen Champagner Cocktail bereitet, thut man nur 2 oder 3 Stückchen Eis in das Glas und mischt wie folgt:

2 oder 3 klein zerschlagene Chrystall Eisstücke.

1 oder 2 schöne Schnitte Orange;

PLATE No. 13.

Danziger Goldwasser.

Yolk of a fresh cold Egg

Chartreuse (yellow).

GOLDEN SLIPPER.

MARTINE COCKTAIL.

2 oder 3 schöne Erdbeeren;
1 Stück Würfelzucker;
1 oder 2 dashes Bitters, (Boker's genuine only);
1 feines Stück Ananas;
fülle das Glas mit Champagner;
mische es gut und füge ein kleines Stück Citronenschale hinzu;
Ehe man die Citronenschale hineinlegt, drehe man
dieselbe zierlich mit den Fingern, wodurch man das
in der Schale enthaltene Citronenöl herauspresst,
welches dem Getränk einen picanten Geschmack
giebt. Wenn eine Gesellschaft Herren dieses Getränk bestellt, hat der Bartender zu fragen, welche
Sorte Champagner gewünscht wird. Eine kleine
Flasche Champagner ist hinreichend für drei Cocktails. Ferner möchte ich bemerken, dass der Bartender den Zucker mit einer Zuckerzange, und die
Früchte mit einer Fruchtgabel zu hantiren hat.
Diese Regel ist hauptsächlich beim Mischen dieser
Getränke zu beobachten.—(Siehe Illustration, Tafel
No. 4.)

57. Martini Cocktail.
(Gebrauche ein grosses Barglas.)

Fülle das Glas mit feinem Eis;
2 oder 3 dashes Gum Syrup;
2 oder 3 dashes Bitters, (Boker's genuine only);
1 dash Curaçoa;
$1/2$ Weinglas Old Tom Gin;
$1/2$ Weinglas Vermouth;
mische dieses gut auf mit einem Barlöffel und seihe
es in ein feines Cocktail Glas, presse ein Stückchen
Citronenschale hinein und servire.—(Siehe Illustrationen, Tafel No. 13.)

58. Champagne Sour.
(Gebrauche ein Fancy Sour Glas.)

1 Stück Würfelzucker;
2 dashes frish ausgepressten Citronensaft;
fülle das Glas langsam mit Champagner, lege etwas

10

feingeschnittene Früchte, wie Trauben, Erdbeeren, Orange, etc., etc., hinein, mische dieses gut auf und servire. Man mische behutsam da der Champagner sehr moussirt.—(Siehe Illustration, Tafel No. 5.

59. Morning Glory Fizz.
(Gebrauche ein grosses Barglas.

In jedem feinem Barroom ist es Regel, dass man das Eiweiss separat vom Dotter in einer Flasche hält, welche immer kalt gestellt werden muss. Mische wie folgt:

1 Eiweiss;
$^3/_4$ Esslöffel voll Zucker;
1 oder 2 dashes Citronensaft;
2 oder 3 dashes Limesaft;
3 oder 4 dashes Absinth; löse dieses mit ein wenig Wasser auf;
$^3/_4$ Glas feines Eis;
1 Weinglas Scotch Whiskey,

schüttele dieses gut in einem Schüttelbecher auf und seihe es in ein ziemlich grosses Glas, fülle das Glas mit Syphon Selters oder Vichy Wasser und servire. Der Verfasser dieses Buches empfiehlt dieses Getränk als einen feinen Morgentrank, da es den Appetit reizt und die Nerven beruhigt.—(Siehe Illustration, Tafel No. 7.)

60. Champagne Julep.
(Gebrauche ein Fancy Julep Glas.

Nimm mit der Zange ein Stück Würfelzucker, und placire dieses und einen langen Zweig Krausemünze in das Glas, dann giesse man den Champagner sehr langsam in das Glas, lege ein Stückchen Orange und Erdbeeren hinein, mische und servire.

Das obige Getränk braucht nicht so lange gemischt zu werden wie andere Juleps, indem der Champagner sehr leicht moussirt, und in Folge dessen über den Rand des Glases laufen würde.—(Siehe Illustration, Tafel No. 14.)

61. Manhattan Cocktail.

(Gebrauche ein grosses Barglas.)

Fülle das Glas mit Eis;
2 or 3 dashes Gum Syrup;
1 oder 2 dashes Bitters; (Boker's genuine only);
1 dash Curaçoa (oder Absinthe wenn es verlangt
    wird);
$^1/_2$ Weinglas Whiskey;
$^1/_2$ Weinglas Vermouth;
mische es gut auf, seihe in ein Fancy Cocktail Glas,
presse ein Stückchen Citronenschale hinein und servire. Betreffs des Absinths richte man sich nach
den Geschmack des Gastes. Dies ist heutzutage ein
wohlbekanntes und viel verlangtes Getränk.

62. Curacoa Punch.

(Gebrauche ein grosses Barglas.)

$^1/_2$ Esslöffel voll feiner Zucker;
2 oder 3 dashes Citronensaft;
$^1/_2$ Weinglas Wasser; löse dieses mit einem Bar-
    löffel gut anf, und fülle das Glas mit zer-
    schlagenem Eis;
$^1/_2$ Weinglas Brandy;
1 Weinglas Curaçoa, (roth);
$^1/_2$ Ponyglas Jamaica Rum;
mische es gut, und garnire mit Weintrauben, Orange,
Ananas und Erdbeeren in geschmackvoller Weise,
und servire mit Strohhalm. Wenn richtig gemischt
ist dies ein sehr wohlschmeckendes Getränk.—(Siehe
Illustration, Tafel No. 12.

63. Mint Julep.

(Gebrauche ein grosses Barglas.)

1 Esslöffel voll feiner Zucker;
$^1/_2$ Weinglas Wasser oder Syphon Selters;
3 oder 4 Zweige frische Krausemünze;
presse die Krausemünze mit einem Barlöffel, bis das
darin enthaltene Oel vollständig absorbirt ist, dann

entferne die Blätter und Stengel und fülle das Glas
mit fein zerschlagenem Eis;
1¹/₂ Weinglas Cognac;
mische oder schüttele dieses tüchtig auf, dann nehme
4 oder 5 frische Krausemünzezweige und placire
diese in bouquetartiger Weise über dem Glase.
Garnire es in geschmackvoller Weise mit Orangen
Ananas, Trauben und Erdbeeren, überstreue dieses
mit ein wenig feinem Zucker, und giesse einige
Tropfen Jamaica Rum darauf; servire mit Strohhalm. Dieses Getränk ist nicht nur in diesem
Lande, sondern in allen Theilen der Welt bekannt
unter dem Namen Mint Julep.—(Siehe Illustration,
Tafel No. 8.

64. Pousse Cafe.

(Gebrauche ein Sherrywein Glas.)

Bei der Zubereitung dieses Getränks, welches nicht
allein Lieblingsgetränk der Franzosen sondern auch
aller andern Nationen der Welt ist, muss mit grosser
Sorgfalt verfahren werden, so dass jede Sorte der
verschiedenen Liqueure separat in ihren Farben er-
scheint; um diesem Getränk ein sehr brillantes Aussehen zu geben, muss man also sehr behutsam zu
Werke gehen. Um die Mischung vorzunehmen
empfiehlt der Verfasser ein Sherry Weinglas zu be-
nutzen, da die Verwendung eines solchen in erster
Linie bequemer ist, dann geschäftsmässiger aussieht
und auch das Mischen schneller von Statten geht.
Mische wie folgt:
1/₆ Sherry Weinglas Parfait d'Amour oder Raspberry Syrup;
1/₆ Sherry Weinglas Maraschino;
1/₆ Sherry Weinglas Vanilla (grün);
1/₆ Sherry Weinglas Curaçoa, (roth);
1/₆ Sherry Weinglas Chartreuse (gelb);
1/₆ Sherry Weinglas Cognac;
Mit diesen Sorten Liqueur ist das Glas gefüllt und
kann servirt werden.
Ferner will ich bemerken, dass man bei der Zube-

reitung dieses Getränks ausfinden muss, welche von
den betreffenden Liqueuren die schwersten sind;
man darf nämlich nicht die schweren Sorten auf die
leichten placiren, indem die Gewichte der Liqueure
sehr verschiedenartig sind; z. B. wiegt der französische Curaçoa schwerer als der holländische. In
Folge dessen ist es rathsam für jeden Bartender der
in Barrooms arbeitet wo dieses Getränk vielfach
verlangt wird, die verschiedenen Flaschen in denen
diese Liquöre enthalten sind, in einer ihrem Gewicht
entsprechenden Reihenfolge auf einer Stelle zu
placiren, da dadurch Irrthümer vermieden, sowie
Zeitverlust und Unannehmlichkeiten erspart werden.
Demzufolge kann der Bartender sich nicht immer
nach dieser Illustration richten. Die von mir gebrauchten Liqueure stimmen genau mit dem Gemisch
überein, welches bei dieser Illustration angegeben
ist.—(Siehe Illustration, Tafel No. 6.)

65. Pousse L'Amour.
(Gebrauche ein Sherry Weinglas.)

Dieses altfranzösische Getränk hat einige Aehnlichkeit mit Pousse Cafe, und muss mit ebenso
grosser Vorsicht zubereitet werden. Man gebrauche
wie folgt:

$1/4$ Sherry Weinglas Maraschino;
1 frischer, kalter Eidotter;
$1/4$ Sherry Weinglas Vanilla (grün);
$1/4$ Weinglas Cognac;
Die grösste Vorsicht muss bei der Mischung dieses
Getränks angewendet werden, so dass der Eidotter
ganz bleibt.—(Siehe Illustration, Tafel No. 6.)

66. Brandy Crusta.
(Gebrauche ein grosses Barglas.)

Man nehme eine schöne, saubere Citrone, ungefähr
in der Grösse und in dem Umfange eines Weinglases, schneide beide Enden der Citrone ab und
schäle dann die Citrone, ungefähr wie man einen

Apfel schält, dass die Schale zusammenhängend
bleibt, dann setze die Citronenschale in ein hübsches
Weinglas und tauche den Rand in pulverisirten
Zucker, dann mische man wis folgt:
3 oder 4 dashes Orchard Syrup;
1 oder 2 dashes Bitters, (Bokers genuine only);
4 oder 5 Tropfen Citronensaft;
2 dashes Maraschino;
$^3/_4$ Glas gefüllt mit Eis;
1 Weinglas Cognac;
mische gut mit einem Barlöffel, seihe es in ein Glas,
mit ein wenig Frucht und servire.—(Siehe Illustration, Tafel No. 5.)

67. Fancy Whiskey Smash.
(Gebrauche ein grosses Barglas.)

$^1/_2$ Esslöffel Zucker;
$^1/_2$ Glas Wasser oder Syphon Selters;
3 oder 4 Zweige Krausemünze;
mische gut auf mit einem Barlöffel; fülle das Glas
    mit fein zerschlagenem Eis.
1 Weinglas Whiskey;
mische, seihe in ein Sourglas; garnire mit Früchten.

68. Whiskey Daisy.
(Gebrauche ein grosses Barglas.)

$^1/_2$ Esslöffel feiner Zucker;
2 oder 3 dashes Citronensaft;
1 dash Limesaft;
1 squirt Syphon Selters, löse dieses mit Zucker, Ci-
    tronen und Limesaft gut auf;
$^3/_4$ voll mit fein zerschlagenem Eis;
1 Weinglas guten Whiskey;
$^1/_2$ Ponyglas Chartreuse (gelb);
mische dieses gut mit einem Barlöffel, dann nehme
ein Fancy Glas, und garnire es mit Frucht in geschmackvoller Weise, und seihe die Ingredienzien
hinein und servire. Dies ist ein sehr wohlschmeckendes Getränk, wenn es richtig zubereitet ist.—(Siehe
Illustration, Tafel No. 10.)

69. Champagne Cobbler.
(Gebrauche ein grosses Barglas.)

$^1/_4$ Löffel voll feiner Zucker;
$^1/_4$ Weinglas Syphon Selter; löse dies gut auf;
1 oder 2 Schnitte Orange;
1 oder 2 Schnitte Ananas;
füllt das Glas mit zerschlagenem Eis;
dann fülle das Glas mit Champagner auf, mische gut
mit einem Barlöffel, garnire mit Orange, Ananas,
Erdbeeren, etc. in geschmackvoller Weise. Dieses
Getränk wird nur in solchen Geschäften bereitet, wo
man Champagner an Zapf hält. — Siehe Illustration, Tafel No. 8.)

70. Roman Punch.
(Gebrauche ein grosses Barglas.)

$^1/_2$ Löffel voll feiner Zucker;
$^1/_2$ Weinglas Raspberry Syrup;
2 oder 3 dashes Citronensaft;
löse dieses mit ein wenig Selters auf;
fülle das Glas mit zerschlagenem Eis;
$^1/_4$ Ponyglas Curaçoa;
$^1/_2$ Weinglas Brandy;
$^1/_2$ Ponyglas Jamaica Rum;
mische dieses gut auf mit einem Barlöffel, garnire
mit Orange, Ananas, Trauben, etc., in geschmackvoller Weise und servire. — (Siehe Illustration,
Tafel No. 14.)

71. Golden Slipper.
(Gebrauche ein Sherry Weinglas.)

$^1/_2$ Weinglas Curaçoa (roth);
1 frischer Eidotter;
$^1/_2$ Weinglas Danziger Goldwasser;
Dies ist ein Lieblingsgetränk südamerikanischer
Damen, und muss mit grosser Vorsicht zubereitet
werden, so dass der Eidotter nicht mit den Liquören
zusammenläuft, sondern seine Form behält.—(Siehe
Illustration, Tafel No. 13.

72. Mississippi Punch.
(Gebrauche ein grosses Barglas.)

1 Löffel voll feiner Zucker;
$^1/_2$ Weinglas Wasser oder Syphon Selters;
2 dashes Citronensaft; löse dieses gut auf;
$^1/_2$ Weinglas Jamaica Rum;
$^1/_2$ Weinglas Bourbon Whiskey;
1 Weinglas Brandy;
Fülle das Glas mit zerschlagenem Eis, schüttle gut
auf, garnire in geschmackvoller Weise mit verschie-
denen Fruchtsorten und servire.—(Siehe Illustration,
Tafel No. 12.)

73. Silver Fizz.
(Gebrauche ein grosses Barglas.)

$^1/_2$ Esslöffel voll feiner Zucker;
2 oder 3 dashes Citronensaft;
1 Weinglas Old Tom Gin, löse dieses gut auf, mit
    ein wenig Selters oder Vichy Wasser;
1 Eiweiss;
$^3/_4$ Glas zerschlagenes Eis;
schüttle dieses gründlich auf in einem Schüttelbecher, seihe es in ein ziemlich grosses Bar oder
Fizzglas, fülle das Glas mit Syphon Selters oder
Vichywasser und servire. Dies ist ein sehr wohlschmeckendes Getränk, und muss getrunken werden
sobald es zubereitet ist, weil es sonst den Effect ver-
lieren würde.

74. Brandy Shamperelle.
(Gebrauche ein Sherry Weinglas.)

$^1/_4$ Weinglas Curaçoa (roth);
$^1/_4$ Weinglas Chartreuse (gelb);
$^1/_4$ Weinglas Anisette;
$^1/_4$ Weinglas Kirschwasser oder Brandy, je nach
    Belieben und servire;
Bei Zubereitung dieses Getränks muss besondere
Vorsicht gebraucht werden um zu verhindern, dass
die verschiedenen Liquöre zusammenlaufen.—(Siehe
Illustration, Tafel No. 6.)

PLATE No. 14.

CHAMPAGNE JULEP.   ROMAN PUNCH.

75. Vanilla Punch.

(Gebrauche ein grosses Barglas.)

1 Esslöffel voll Zucker;
2 oder 3 dashes Lime oder Citronensaft;
2 oder 3 dashes Curoçoa, löse es mit ein wenig
    Wasser oder Syphon Selters auf;
fülle das Glas mit zerschlagenem Eis;
1 Ponyglas Brandy;
. 1¹/₂ Weinglas Vanilla;
mische dieses gut mit einem Barlöffel; garnire in
geschmackvoller Weise mit Früchten und servire
mit Strohhalm.

76. Knickerbocker.

(Gebrauche ein grosses Barglas.)

2 Esslöffel Raspberry Syrup (Himbeersaft);
2 dashes Citronensaft;
1 Schnitt Ananas;
1 Schnitt Orange;
1 Weinglas St Croix Rum;
¹/₂ Weinglas Curaçoa;
Fülle das Glas mit zerschlagenem Eis;
mische oder schüttle tüchtig und garnire mit Früchten; servire mit Strohhalm.

77. Toledo Punch.

(Gebrauche eine Punschbowle.)

Dieser Punsch kann nur für eine Gesellschaft bereitet werden. Der Verfasser des Buches hat diesen
Punsch speciell für ein grosses, feines, amerikani-
sches Etablissement in Chicago componirt und ihm
den Namen "Toledo" beigelegt. Man nimmt:
2 lb. Würfelzucker;
4 oder 5 Flaschen Sodawasser;
4 Citronen (presse solche aus);
1 quart Französischen Cognac;
1 kleines Büschel Wintergrün;
4 Orangen (schneide diese in Scheiben);

1 Ananas (schneide diese in Scheiben);
und placire diese Scheiben in der Punschbowle, auch
Erdbeeren und Trauben; mische die Ingredienzen
mit einem Bar oder Schöpflöffel.
6 Flaschen Champagner;
1 Flasche Brandy;
2 Flaschen Rhein Wein;
1½ Gallon Wasser;
mische dieses gut auf in einer Punschbowle, und
man wird einen der vorzüglisten Punsche haben,
die es überhaupt gibt.

Es ist selbstverständlich, dass dieses Getränk durch
Eis kalt gehalten werden muss, auf dieselbe Art,
wie alle anderen Punschsorten. Ferner gebrauche
bei der Verabreichung dieses Getränkes, ein fancy
Barglas, fülle es mit dem betreffenden Getränk und
füge einem jeden Glas, ein wenig Orange, Ananas,
Erdbeeren, etc., bei, und servire dann.

78. Absinthe Cocktail.
(Gebrauche ein grosses Barglas.)

Fülle das Glas mit zerschlagenem Eis;
3 oder 4 dashes Gum Syrup;
1 dash Bitters; (Boker's genuine only);
1 dash Anisette;
¼ Weinglas Wasser;
¾ Weinglas Absinthe;
schüttele gründlich, und so lange, bis es sich zu
einer Eismasse bildet, seihe es in ein fancy Cocktail
Glas; füge ein Stück Citronenschale darauf und
servire es.

Dieses Getränk wird nicht nur von Franzosen,
sondern auch von Amerikanern vielfach getrunken,
es ist ein sehr Appetit erregendes und wohlschmeckendes Getränk. Uebrigens ist es zu beachten, dass
man stets den ächten Absinthe dazu verwenden
muss.

79. Sherry Cobbler.
(Gebrauche ein grosses Barglass.)

$^1/_2$ Esslöffel feiner Zucker;
$^1/_2$ Weinglas Wasser, löse gut auf mit einem Barlöffel;
fülle das Glas mit Crystall Eis; dann fülle das
Glas mit Sherry Wein;
mische dieses gründlich mit einem Barlöffel, und
garnire mit Trauben, Ananas, Erdbeeren, etc., in
geschmackvoller Weise, und servire.
Dieses ist ohne Zweifel ein Lieblings-Getränk
in diesem Lande, sowohl für Damen als Herren.

80. Sherry Flip.
(Gebrauche ein grosses Barglas.)

1 frisches Ei;
$^1/_2$ Esslöffel voll Zucker;
$^1/_2$ Glas zerschlagenes Eis;
$1^1/_2$ Weinglas Sherry Wein;
schüttele gut in einem Schüttelbecher, seihe es in
ein fancy Barglas, streue ein wenig Muscatnuss darauf
und servire.
Dieses ist ein ebenso wohlschmeckendes wie
stärkendes Getränk und hauptsächlich empfehlens-
werth für schwache Personen. (Siehe Illustration,
Tafel No. 15.)

81. Brandy Punch.
(Gebrauche ein grosses Barglas.)

$^3/_4$ Esslöffel voll feiner Zucker;
Einige Tropfen Ananas Syrup;
1 oder 2 dashes Citronensaft;
1 oder 2 dashes Limesaft;
1 squirt Syphon Selters;
mische dieses gut, fülle das Glas auf mit zerschlagenem Eis;
$1^1/_2$ Weinglas alten Cognac oder Brandy;
mische dieses gründlich auf mit einem Barlöffel und

giesse mehreren Tropfen Jamaica Rum darauf; garnire es in geschmackvoller Weise mit Orange, Ananas, Erdbeeren, etc., und servire es.

82. St. Charles Punch.
(Gebrauche ein grosses Barglas.)

1 Esslöffel voll feiner Zucker;
2 oder 3 dashes Citronensaft;
1 squirt Syphon Selters; löse dieses gut auf, und
füge hinzu:
1 Weinglas Port Wein;
1 Ponyglas Brandy;
$^1/_2$ Weinglas Curaçoa;
Fülle das Glas mit zerschlagenem Eis;
mische dieses gründlich mit einem Barlöffel, garnire
mit Orange, Ananas, Erdbeeren, etc., und servire.

83. Egg Nogg.
(Gebrauche ein grosses Barglas.)

1 frisches Ei;
$^3/_4$ Esslöffel voll feiner Zucker;
$^1/_2$ Glas feines Eis;
1 Ponyglas St. Croix oder Jamaica Rum;
1 Weinglas Brandy;
Fülle das Glas mit guter Milch;
schüttele dieses gründlich zusammen, und seihe es
in ein grosses feines Barglas, streue ein wenig Muscatnuss darauf, und servire.
Es ist die Pflicht eines Bartender's den Gast zu
fragen, ob er zu diesem Getränk St. Croix oder
Jamaica Rum gebrauchen soll, da dieses von dem
Geschmack des Gastes abhängt.

84. White Lion.
(Gebrauche ein grosses Barglass)

1 Esslöffel voll feiner Zucker;
2 oder 3 dashes Lime oder Citronensaft;
1 squirt Syphon Selters;
mische dieses gut auf, mit einen Barlöffel;

$^1/_2$ Ponyglas Raspberry Syrup;
Fülle das Glas mit feinem Eis;
$^1/_2$ Ponyglas Curaçoa;
1 Weinglas St. Croix Rum;
mische dieses gut, und garnire es in geschmackvoller Weise, mit Orange, Ananas, Erdbeeren, etc.,
und servire.

85. Baltimore Egg Nogg.
(Gebrauche ein grosses Barglas.)

1 frisches Eidotter;
$^3/_4$ Esslöffel feiner Zucker;
füge ein wenig pulversirten Zimmt hinzu und
mische dieses gut mit einem Barlöffel;
$^1/_2$ Ponyglas Brandy;
3 oder 4 kleine Eisstücke;
$^1/_4$ Ponyglas Jamaica Rum;
1 Weinglas Madeira Wein;
Fülle das Glas mit Milch;
schüttele und seihe es in ein grosses Barglas, streue
ein wenig Muscatnuss darüber, und servire.

86. Fancy Brandy Cocktail.
(Gebrauche ein grosses Barglas.)

$^3/_4$ Glas fein zerschlagenes Eis;
2 oder 3 dashes Gum Syrup;
$1^1/_2$ dashes Bitters; (Boker's genuine only)
$1^1/_2$ dashes Curaçoa;
1 Glas Brandy; (Cognac)
mische dieses tüchtig mit einem Barlöffel, seihe es
in ein fancy Cocktail Glas, presse ein Stück Citronenschale hinein, und füge 1 squirt Champagner
hinzu, und servire; das heisst wo Champagner am
Zapf ist.

87. Whiskey Crusta.
(Gebrauche ein grosses Barglas)

Man nehme eine schöne, saubere Citrone, ungefähr in der Grösse und im Umfange eines Weinglases, schneide beide Enden der Citrone ab mit

einem Messer, und schäle dann die ganze Citrone mit
einen Schnitt, so wie man einen Apfel scnält, dann
setze die Citronenschale in ein hübsches Weinglas,
und tupfe dasselbe mit dem Rande in pulverisirten
Zucker. Dann mische folgendermassen:
1 Ponyglas Orchard Syrup;
1 oder 2 dashes Bitters; Boker's genuine only)
1 dash Citronensaft;
2 dashes Maraschino;
$1/2$ Glas feines Eis;
$3/4$ Glas Whiskey;
mische dieses gut auf mit einen Barlöffel, seihe
dasselbe in das die Citronenschale enthaltende Weinglas und füge ein kleines Stück Ananas, Erdbeeren,
Orange, etc., hinzu, und servire.

88. Fancy Brandy Smash.
(Gebrauche ein grosses Barglass.)

$1/2$ Esslöffel feiner Zucker;
$1/2$ Weinglass Wasser oder Syphon Selters;
3 oder 4 Zweige frische Krausemünze;
mische dies gründlich mit einem Barlöffel;
$1/2$ Glas feines Eis;
1 Weinglas Brandy (Cognac);
mische dieses gut auf, seihe es in ein sour oder
fancy Barglas, garnire in geschmackvoller Weise
mit klein geschnittenen Früchten und Beeren, und
servire es. (Siehe Illustration, Tafel No. 9.)

89. Sherry Wine Punch.
(Gebrauche ein grosses Barglas.)

$1/2$ Weinglas Orchard Syrup;
1 dash Citronensaft;
fülle das Glas mit feinem Eis;
$1^1/2$ Weinglas Sherry Wein;
mische dieses gut auf mit einem Barlöffel und
garnire mit Orange, Ananas, Erdbeeren, etc., giesse
ein wenig Claret Wein darauf, und servire.

90. Brandy Fix.
(Gebrauche ein grosses Barglas.)

$^1/_2$ Esslöffel feiner Zucker;
2 oder 3 dashes Lime oder Citronensaft;
$^1/_2$ Ponyglas Ananas Syrup, (pineapple);
1 oder 2 dashes Curaçoa (grün);
1 dash Syphon Selters; mische dieses gut auf;
Fülle das Glas mit feinem Eis;
1 Weinglas Brandy;
mische dieses tüchtig mit einem Barlöffel, garnire in geschmackvoller Weise mit in Stücke geschnittener Frucht und servire.

91. Claret Punch.
(Gebrauche ein grosses Barglas.)

$^3/_4$ Esslöffel feiner Zucker;
1 squirt Syphon Selters;
$^1/_2$ dash Citronensaft; d. h. wenn der Wein nicht
   zu sauer ist; löse dieses gut auf;
fülle das Glas mit feinem Eis;
$1^1/_2$ Glas Claret Wein;
mische dieses tüchtig mit einem Barlöffel, garnire in geschmackvoller Weise, mit Orange, Ananas, Erdbeeren, etc., und servire.

92. Knickerbein.
(Gebrauche ein Sherry Weinglas.)

$^1/_3$ Weinglas Vanilla;
1 frischer Eidotter;
füge auf dieses ein wenig Benedictine;
$^1/_3$ Weinglas Kirschwasser oder Cognac;
3 oder 4 Tropfen Bitters, (Boker's genuine only);
Besondere Vorsicht muss bei diesem Getränk beobachtet werden, dass beim Eingiessen der resp. Liquöre diese nicht in einander laufen, sondern im Glase getrennt bleiben, da dies dem Getränk ein appetitliches Aussehen verleiht. Der Eidotter muss aus demselben Grunde ganz in das Glas gebracht werden und darf nicht verlaufen.

93. Santinas Pousse Cafe.
(Gebrauche ein Sherry Weinglas.)

$^1/_3$ Weinglas Maraschino;
$^1/_3$ Weinglas Curaçoa, (roth):
$^1/_3$ Weinglas franz. Cognac und servire.
Vorsicht bei Bereitung muss gebraucht werden,
damit die verschiedenen Liquöre nicht zusammen-
laufen. Dieses Getränk ist vorzüglich nach dem
Genusse von schwarzem Caffee.

94. Sauterne Cobbler.
(Gebrauche ein grosses Barglas.)

$^1/_2$ Esslöffel feiner Zucker;
$^1/_2$ Weinglas Orchard Syrup;
$^1/_4$ Weinglas Syphon Selters, löse dieses gut auf;
fülle das Glas mit feinem Eis;
$1^1/_2$ Weinglas Sauterne Wein;
mische dieses gut auf mit einem Barlöffel, garnire
in geschmackvoller Weise mit Orange, Ananas, etc.,
und servire

95. Milk Punch.
(Gebrauche ein grosses Barglas.)

$^3/_4$ Esslöffel voll Zucker;
$^1/_3$ Glas feines Eis;
1 Weinglas Brandy;
$^1/_2$ Weinglas St. Croix Rum;
fülle das Glas mit Milch;
schüttle tüchtig in einem Schüttelbecher, seihe in
ein grosses Glas, streue ein wenig Muscatnuss darauf
und servire es.

96. Faivre's Pousse Cafe.
(Gebrauche ein Sherry Weinglas)

$^1/_3$ Glas Benedictine;
$^1/_3$ Glas Curaçoa; (roth)
$^1/_3$ Glas Kirschwasser oder Cognac;
3 oder 4 Tropfen Bitters; (Boker's genuine only)
und servire.

SHERRY FLIP.

Sei beim Eingiessen der verschiedenen Sorten
Liqueure sehr behutsam, damit sich solche nicht
vermischen, sondern schichtenweise im Glase stehen.

97. How to Mix Absinthe.
(Gebrauche ein Absinthe Glas.)

Ehe der Bartender dieses Getränk bereitet, muss er
den Gast fragen auf welche Art, ob auf französische,
italienische, deutsche oder amerikanische, er das
Getränk bereitet haben will, da diese 4 Arten bei
den betreffenden Mischungen bedeutend von einander abweichen.—Mische wie folgt für französische
Art:

Nehme den Untertheil des Absintheglases, stelle
diesen auf den Counter, fülle 1 Ponyglas mit
Absinthe, stelle solches in den Untertheil des Absinthe Glases, nehme dann den Obertheil des Absinthe Glases, welcher eine bowlenartige Form und
eine kleine runde Oeffnung am Boden hat, lege
3 oder 4 kleine zerschlagene Stücke Eis in diesen
und fülle die Bowle mit Wasser, hebe sie dann hoch
und lasse das Wasser langsam in den Absinthe
laufen, bis das Getränk eine milchartige Farbe
bekommt. Entferne das Ponyglas, giesse die Mischung in ein grosses Barglas, und servire.

98. American Style of mixing Absinthe.
(Gebrauche ein grosses Barglas.)

$^3/_4$ Glas feines Eis;
6 oder 7 dashes Gum Syrup;
1 Ponyglas Absinthe;
2 Weinglas Wasser;
schüttele dieses mittelst eines Schüttelbechers gut
auf, seihe es in ein grosses Barglas, und servire.

99. Italian Style of mixing Absinthe.
(Gebrauche ein grosses Barglas.)

1 Ponyglas Absinthe;
2 oder 3 Eisstücke;
2 oder 3 dashes Maraschino;

11

$^1/_2$ Ponyglas Anisette;
giesse das Eiswasser langsam in das Barglas, welches
die Ingredienzien enthält; mische diese gut auf mit
einem Barlöffel und servire.

100. German or Swiss Style of mixing Absinthe.
(Gebrauche ein grosses Barglas.)

Dieses wird auf einfache Weise zubereitet, indem
man 1 Ponyglas Absinthe in ein grosses Barglas
giesst, und dieses mit kaltem Wasser auffüllt und
so wird es gewöhnlich von dem betreffenden Bartender servirt.

101. Golden Fizz.
(Gebrauche ein grosses Barglas.)

$^3/_4$ Esslöffel feiner Zucker;
2 oder 3 dashes Citronensaft;
1 Weinglas Whiskey; (oder Tom Gin wenn es
   verlangt wird);
1 frisches Eidotter;
$^3/_4$ Glas zerschlagenes Eis;
schüttele dieses gut auf mittelst eines Schüttelbechers, und seihe es in ein ziemlich grosses Bar
oder Fizz Glas; fülle dieses auf mit Syphon Vichy
Wasser, mische mit einem Barlöffel, und servire.

102. Vermouth Cocktail.
(Gebrauche ein grosses Barglas.)

$^3/_4$ Glas zerschlagenes Eis;
4 oder 5 dashes Gum Syrup;
1 oder 2 dashes Bitters; (Boker's genuine only)
1 Weinglas Vermouth;
2 dashes Maraschino;
mische dieses gut mit einem Barlöffel, seihe es in ein
Cocktailglas füge ein kleines Stück Citronenschale
zu, und servire es.

103. Selters Lemonade.
(Gebrauche ein grosses Barglass.)

$1^1/_2$ Esslöffel voll Zucker;
6 oder 8 dashes Citronensaft;

4 oder 5 Eisstücke;
fülle das Glas mit Syphon Selters; mische dieses
gut auf mittelst eines Barlöffels. Sollte der Gast
importirtes Selters Wasser verlangen, so gebrauche
man dieses anstatt des Syphon Selters Wasser.

Dieses Getränk ist besonders zu empfehlen in
heisser Jahreszeit und es beruhigt zugleich erregte
Nerven.

104. Port Wine Punch.

(Gebrauche ein grosses Barglas.)

$^1/_2$ Esslöffel Zucker;
$^1/_2$ Esslöffel Orchard Syrup;
1 oder 2 dashes Citronensaft;
$^1/_2$ Weinglas Wasser;
mische dieses gut auf;
Fülle das Glas mit feinem Eis;
$1^1/_2$ Weinglas Portwein;
mische gut auf mit einem Barlöffel, garnire in geschmackvoller Weise mit Orange, Ananas, Erdbeeren
etc., und servire.

105. Whiskey Julep.

(Gebrauche ein grosses Barglas.)

$^3/_4$ Esslöffel Zucker;
$^1/_2$ Weinglas Wasser oder Syphon Selters;
3 oder 4 Zweige Krausemünze (Mint), presse dies
    mit einem Löffel tüchtig, so dass das darin
    enthaltene Oel sich löst;
fülle das Glas mit feingeschlagenem Eis;
1 Weinglas Whiskey;
mische dieses tüchtig mit einem Barlöffel und garnire es mit Krausemünze, die Stengel nach unten,
Orange, Ananas, Citrone und Erdbeeren in geschmackvoller Weise, streue etwas pulverisirten
Zucker darüber und giesse einige Tropfen Jamaica
Rum auf das Ganze und servire es mit Strohhalm.

106. Brandy Flip.
(Gebrauche ein grosses Barglas.)

1 frisches Ei;
³/₄ Esslöffel Zucker;
³/₄ Glas feines Eis;
1 Weinglas Cognac;
schüttele alles gut in einem Schüttelbecher durch-
einander und seihe es in ein Flip oder sonstiges
hübsches Barglas, streue ein wenig Muscatnuss darüber und servire.

107. St. Croix Rum Punch.
(Gebrauche ein grosses Barglas.)

1 Esslöffel Zucker;
3 oder 4 dashes Lime oder Citronensaft;
¹/₂ Weinglas Wasser; löse gut auf;
¹/₄ Ponyglas Jamaica Rum;
1 Weinglas St. Croix Rum;
fülle das Glas mit feinem Eis;
mische dieses gut auf mittelst eines Barlöffels, garnire mit Frucht in geschmackvoller Weise und servire mit Strohhalm.

108. General Harrison Egg Nogg.
(Gebrauche ein grosses Barglas.)

1 frisches Ei;
¹/₄ Esslöffel Zucker;
3 oder 4 Eisstücke;
fülle das Glas mit Apfelwein (Cider);
schüttle dieses vermittelst eines Schüttelbechers gut
auf, seihe es in ein grosses Glas, streue ein wenig
Muscatnuss darauf und servire. Dieses Getränk ist
sehr wohlschmeckend und hauptsächlich im süd-
lichen America sehr beliebt.

109. Tip Top Punch.
(Gebrauche ein grosses Barglas.)

3 oder 4 Eisstücke;
1 Ponyglas Brandy;
1 Stück Würfelzucker;

1 oder 2 Schnitte Orange;
1 oder 2 Schnitte Ananas;
2 oder 3 Tropfen Citronensaft;
fülle das Glas auf mit Champagner, mische dieses
gut auf mit einen Barlöffel, garnire mit Trauben,
Erdbeeren, etc., und servire.

110. Medford Rum Sour.
(Gebrauche ein grosses Barglas.)

$^1/_2$ Esslöffel Zucker;
3 oder 4 dashes Citronensaft;
1 squirt Syphon Selters, löse dieses gut auf;
1 Weinglas Medford Rum;
fülle das Glas $^3/_4$ mit zerschlagenem Eis;
mische dieses mit einem Barlöffel gut auf, seihe es
in ein Sourglas, garnire mit Citrone, Ananas und
Orange, und servire.

111. The Old Delaware Fishing Punch.
(Gebrauche ein grosses Barglas.)

1 Esslöffel Zucker;
1 oder 2 dashes Citronensaft;
1 oder 2 dashes Limesaft, löse dies gut auf mit ein
      wenig Wasser;
fülle das Glas mit feinem Eis;
1 Weinglas St. Croix Rum;
1 Ponyglas alten Cognac;
mische dieses gut auf mit einem Barlöffel, garnire
mit Saisonfrucht und servire mit Strohhalm.

112. Tom Collins.
(Gebrauche ein extra grosses Barglass.)

$^3/_4$ Esslöffel voll Zucker;
3 oder 4 dashes Lime oder Citronensaft;
3 oder 4 Eisstücke;
1 Weinglas Old Tom Gin;
1 Flasche plain Sodawasser;
mische dieses gut auf mit einem Barlöffel, entferne
das Eis und servire. Vorsicht muss beim Mischen
dieses Getränks gebraucht werden, damit es nicht
über das Glas schäumt.

113. Apple Jack Sour.
(Gebrauche ein grosses Barglas.)

$^1/_2$ Esslöffel Zucker;
2 oder 3 dashes Citronensaft;
1 squirt Syphon Selters, löse dieses gut auf;
$^3/_4$ Glas zerschlagenes Eis;
1 Weinglas Apple Jack;
mische dieses gut mit einem Barlöffel und seihe es
in ein Sourglas, garnire dieses mit klein geschnittenen Saisonfrüchten und servire.

114. Gin Fizz.
(Gebrauche ein grosses Barglas)

$^1/_2$ Esslöffel Zucker;
3 oder 4 dashes Citronensaft;
$^1/_2$ Glas zerschlagenes Eis;
1 Weinglas Old Tom Gin;
mische dieses gut auf mit einem Barlöffel, seihe es
in ein ziemlich grosses Bar oder Fizz-Glas, fülle
es dann mit Syphon Vichy oder Selters, mische gut
auf und servire. Dieses Getränk soll gleich nach
Bereitung getrunken werden, da es sonst Kraft und
Wohlgeschmack verliert.

115. Ale Sangaree.
(Gebrauche ein grosses Barglas.)

1 Theelöffel voll Zucker;
$^1/_2$ Weinglas Wasser, löse dieses gut auf;
fülle das Glas mit Ale, streue ein wenig Muscatnuss
darauf und servire. Es ist gebräuchlich die Gäste
zu fragen, welche Sorte Ale, ob altes, neues oder
Mixed Ale, sie wünschen. Ferner lasse man das
Ale beim Mischen nicht überlaufen. Die Temperatur des Getränkes soll nicht zu kalt aber auch nicht
zu warm sein.

116. Blue Blazer.
(Gebrauche einen Mug mit Henkel.)

$^1/_2$ Ponyglas Honig oder Rock Candy;
$^1/_3$ Weinglas Syrup;

1 Weinglas Scotch Whiskey;
löse gut auf mit ein wenig heissem Wasser, setze
dieses über ein Feuer und lasse es aufkochen, dann
schütte es aus der Pfanne in die Mugs und brenne es
mit einem Streichholz an, giesse es dann schnell von
einem Mug zum andern in langen Strömen, streue ein
wenig Muscatnuss darüber und servire. Der Bartender muss beim Umgiessen des Getränkes Achtung
geben, dass er sich nicht verbrenne, indem das Ganze
eine Flamme ist.

117. Bowl of Egg Nogg for a New Year's Party.

(Gebrauche eine Punchbowle.)

Betreffs der zu bereitenden Quantität dieses Getränkes richtet man sich je nach der Zahl der Gäste.
Folgendes Recept giebt die Maasse für ungefähr
3 Gallonen Egg Nogg:

2½ Pfund pulverisirter Zucker; ;
20 frische Eier:
separire das Eiweiss sorgfältig vom Dotter, und
    schlage letzteren so dünnflüssig wie Wasser;
Mische dieses mit den Zucker gut zusammen;
2 Quart guten alten Cognac;
1½ Pint Jamaica Rum;
2 Gallonen gute Milch;
mische dieses gut zusammen, und während dem
Eingiessen der Milch, welche langsam den anderen
Ingredientien zugegossen werden muss, rühre man
die ganze Masse mittelst eines langen Löffels oder
Ladles fortwährend um. Dann schlage man das Eiweiss mit dem Schneeschläger, bis es steif wie Schnee
ist, und placire es stückchen- und schichtenweise auf
den gemischten Egg Nogg. Beim Serviren dieses
Getränkes bediene man sich eines schönen Glases
und lege auf jedes gefüllte Glas ein Stückchen ge-
schlagenes Eiweiss, bestreue dasselbe mit etwas
Muscatnuss und servire. Auf diese Weise hat man
einen ausgezeichneten Egg Nogg der sehr zu empfehlen ist für Neujahrsgäste.

118. John Collins.

³/₄ Esslöffel Zucker:
2 oder 3 dashes Citronensaft;
2 dashes Limesaft;
4 oder 5 Eisstücke;
1 Weinglas Holland Gin;
1 Flasche plain Sodawasser;
giesse dieses zu den andern Ingredientien, und
mische es tüchtig mit einem Barlöffel auf, entferne
das Eis, und servire es.

Vorsicht muss beim Mischen insofern gebraucht
werden, dass der Schaum nicht über das Glas läuft.

119. East India Cocktail.

Fülle das Glas mit zerschlagenem Eis;
1 Theelöffel Curaçoa (roth);
1 Theelöffel Ananas Syrup;
2 oder 3 dashes Bitters; (Boker's genuine only)
2 dashes Maraschino;
1 Weinglas Brandy;
mische dieses gut mit einem Barlöffel, seihe dieses
in ein fancy Cocktailglas, füge ein kleines Stück
Citronenschale hinzu, und servire.

120. Soda Lemonade.

1 Esslöffel Zucker;
6 oder 8 dashes Citronensaft;
3 oder 4 Eisstücke;
1 Flasche plain Sodawasser;
mische dieses tüchtig auf mit einem Barlöffel, entferne das Eis, und servire es.

Beim Oeffnen der Flasche Sodawasser ist zu
beachten, dass solches stets unter dem Counter
geschieht, damit nicht etwa bei zu starkem Moussee
die Gäste bespritzt werden.

121. Old Style Whiskey Smash.
(Gebrauche ein extra grosses Whiskeyglas.)

$^1/_4$ Esslöffel Zucker;
$^1/_2$ Weinglas Wasser;
3 oder 4 Zweige Krausemünze;
Presse und löse dies gut auf mit einem Barlöffel,
 fülle das Glas mit klein zerschlagenem Eis;
1 Weinglas Whiskey;
lege einige kleine Fruchtstücke hinzu, mische dieses
gut auf, und servire es.

122. Soda Cocktail.
(Gebrauche ein grosses Barglas.)

4 oder 5 kleine Eisstücke;
5 oder 6 dashes Bitters; (Boker's genuine only)
1 oder 2 Schnitte Orange;
fülle das Glas mit lemon Sodawasser;
mische dieses gut auf mit einem Barlöffel, und thue
einen Barlöffel voll feinen Zucker darauf, und servire.

123. How to mix Tom and Jerry.
(Gebrauche eine Punschbowle.)

Bei Bereitung von Tom und Jerry richtet sich die
Quantität ganz nach dem Bedarfe des betreffenden
Geschäftes und müssen die zu verwendenden Eier
stets frisch und kalt sein. Man nehme 2 Gefässe
oder Bowlen und trenne das Eiweiss von dem Dotter so behutsam, das jedes für sich separat in die
betreffende Bowle gebracht wird. Man schlage das
Eiweiss mit einem sogenannten Schneeschläger so
lange bis das Eiweiss steif wie Schnee geworden ist.
Dann füge einen bis anderhalb Esslöffel voll fein
pulversirten Zucker für je 1 Ei hinzu und mische
dieses mittelst des Schneeschlägers tüchtig zu einem
Teig, dann schlage man den Eidotter so lange bis
er dünnflüssig wie Wasser wird und schütte diesen
in den Eiweissteig und schlage das Ganze tüchtig
zusammen, so dass es einen leichten lockeren Teig
bildet.

124. How to deal out Tom and Jerry.
(Gebrauche ein Tom und Jerry Mug.)

2 Esslöffel voll des gemischten Teigs;
1 Weinglass Cognac;
1 Ponyglas Jamaica Rum;
fülle das Glas oder den Mug mit heissem Wasser
oder heisser Milch, je nach dem Wunsche der Gäste
und mische es auf mit einem Barlöffel; dann nehme
man ein zweites Glas oder Mug und giesse das Getränk ungefähr 4 bis 5 Mal von einem Glas ins
andere in langen Strömen, streue dann ein wenig
Muscatnuss darauf, und servire.

125. Egg Lemonade.
(Gebrauche ein grosses Barglas.)

1 frisches Ei;
1 Löffel Zucker;
7 oder 8 dashes Citronensaft;
$^3/_4$ Glas zerschlagenes Eis;
fülle das Glas mit Wasser;
schüttele dieses in einem Schüttelbecher gut auf,
seihe es in ein grosses Barglas, und servire.

126. St. Croix Sour.
(Gebrauche ein grosses Barglas.)

$^1/_2$ Esslöffel Zucker;
3 oder 4 dashes Citronensaft;
2 squirt Syphon Selters;
löse dieses gut auf;
$^3/_4$ Glas zerschlagenes Eis;
1 Weinglas St. Croix Rum;
mische dieses tüchtig mit einem Barlöffel, seihe
es in ein Sourglas, garnire mit klein geschnittenen
Saisonfrüchten, und servire.

127. Egg Milk Punch.
(Gebrauche ein grosses Barglas.)

1 frisches Ei;
$^3/_4$ Esslöffel voll Zucker;
$^1/_4$ Glas zerschlagenes Eis;

1 Weinglas Brandy;
1 Ponyglas St. Croix Rum;
fülle das Glas mit guter Milch, und schüttele es in
einem Schüttelbecher, seihe es in ein grosses Barglas, streue ein wenig Muscatnuss darauf, und
servire.

128. Whiskey Cobbler.

(Gebrauche ein grosses Barglas.)

$^1/_2$ Esslöffel voll Zucker;
$1^1/_2$ Theelöffel Ananas Syrup;
$^1/_2$ Weinglas Wasser oder Syphon Selters;
löse dies gut auf mit einen Löffel;
fülle das Glas mit fein zerschlagenem Eis;
1 Weinglas Whiskey;
mische dieses gut auf mit einem Barlöffel, garnire
es in geschmackvoller Weise mit Orange, Ananas,
Weintrauben, und servire es.

129. Sherry and Egg.

(Gebrauche ein Whiskeyglas.)

Bei Herstellung dieses Getränkes ist es Regel,
erst ein Weniges vom Sherrywein in das betreffende
Glas zu giessen; dieses verhütet nämlich das An-
kleben des Eies am Boden des Glases, dann nehme
man 1 frisches kaltes Ei, schlage dieses in's Glas und
reiche es dann nebst der Flasche Sherrywein dem
Gaste zur eigenen Bedienung. Man muss stets den
Gast fragen, ob er das ganze Ei wünscht oder nur
den Dotter.

130. St. Croix Crusta.

(Gebrauche ein grosses Barglas.)

Man nehme eine schöne, saubere Citrone, ungefähr
in der Grösse und im Umfange eines Weinglases,
schneide beide Enden der Citrone mit einem Messer
ab und schäle dann die ganze Citrone mit einem
Schnitt, wie man einen Apfel shält, dann placire die
Citronenschale in ein hübsches Weinglas und tupfe

dasselbe mit dem Rande in pulverisirten Zucker;
dann mische folgendes:

3 oder 4 dashes Orchard Syrup;
1 dash Bitters, (Boker's genuine only);
$\frac{1}{2}$ Glas fein zerschlagenes Eis;
$\frac{1}{2}$ dash Citronensaft;
2 dashes Maraschino;
1 Weinglas St. Croix Rum;
mische dieses gut auf mit einem Barlöffel, seihe es
dann in das die Citronenschale enthaltende Weinglas, garnire mit Frucht und servire.

131. Rhine Wine Cobbler.
(Gebrauche ein grosses Barglas.)

$1\frac{1}{2}$ Esslöffel Zucker;
$\frac{1}{2}$ Weinglas Wasser oder Syphon Selters;
löse gut auf mit einem Barlöffel, fülle das Glas
mit feinem Eis;
$1\frac{1}{2}$ Weinglas Rheinwein
mische dieses gut, garnire mit Orange, Weintrauben,
Ananas, Erdbeeren etc., und servire mit Strohhalm.

132. Hot Spiced Rum.
(Gebrauche ein Heisswasser-Glas.)

1 oder 2 Stück Würfelzucker;
$\frac{1}{2}$ Theelöffel gemischte Gewürze;
vermische dieses gut mit etwas heissem Wasser:
1 Weinglas Jamaica Rum;
fülle das Glas mit heissem Wasser;
mische es gut mit einem Barlöffel, streue ein wenig
Muscatnuss darüber und servire. Sollte der Gast
ein klein wenig Butter zu diesem Getränk verlangen
dann ist besonders zu beachten, dass nur die beste
Qualität und vollständig frische Butter verwendet
wird. Dieses Getränk ist Halzleidenden besonders
zu empfehlen.

133. May Wine Punch.
(Gebrauche eine Punchbowle.)

Man nehme einen mittelgrossen Büschel frischen
Waldmeister, zerschneide denselben in mehrere

Stücke, lege ihn in ein grosses Barglas, fülle dasselbe
mit Cognac und lasse dies 2 bis 3 Stunden anziehen.
Dann bedecke man den Boden der Bowle mit Stücken
Würfelzucker, giesse über denselben 4 bis 6 Flaschen
plain Sodawasser, schneide 6 Orangen in Schnitte,
$^1/_2$ Ananas in Scheiben, eine genügende Anzahl Erdbeeren, gebe dieses ebenfalls in die Bowle, giesse
dann 8 Flaschen Rhein oder Moselwein, 1 Flasche
Champagner, sowie das Barglas mit Cognac und
Waldmeister über das Ganze, mische dieses gut auf
mit einem grossen Löffel, eise die Bowle in hübscher
Art und Weise nach Vorschrift, und man wird $2^1/_2$
bis 3 Gallonen ausgezeichneten Maitrank haben,
Servire in Weingläsern und sehe, dass jeder Gast
auch etwas Früchte in sein Glas bekommt. Wenn
man dies Getränk zu einer Jahreszeit machen will
wo frischer Waldmeister nicht zu haben ist, nehme
man anstatt desselben Waldmeister Essenz.

134. Whiskey Cocktail.
(Gebrauche ein grosses Barglas.)

$^3/_4$ Glas fein zerschlagenes Eis;
2 oder 3 dashes Gum Syrup;
$1^1/_2$ oder 3 dashes Bitters, (Boker's genuine only);
1 oder 2 dashes Curaçoa;
1 Weinglas Whiskey;
mische gut auf mit einem Barlöffel, seihe es in ein
Cocktail Glas, füge ein kleines Stück Citronenschale
hinzu und servire.

135. Cold Whiskey Sling.
(Gebrauche ein kleines Barglas.)

1 Theelöffel Zucker;
$^1/_2$ Weinglas Wasser, löse dies gut auf;
1 oder 2 Eisstücke;
1 Weinglas Whiskey;
mische dieses gut auf, streue ein wenig Muscatnuss
darüber und servire. Auf Wunsch füge man etwas
Citrone hinzu.

136. Jersey Cocktail.
(Gebrauche ein grosses Barglas.)

1½ Esslöffel voll Zucker;
3 oder 4 Eisstücke;
3 oder 4 dashes Bitters, (Boker's genuine only);
1 Weinglas Aepfelwein (Cider);
mische dieses gut auf mit einem Barlöffel, seihe es
in ein Cocktailglas, füge ein kleines Stück Citronenschale bei und servire. Dies ist ein beliebtes Getränk der Bewohner von Jersey.

137. Kirschwasser Punch.
(Gebrauche ein grosses Barglas.)

½ Esslöffel Zucker;
1 oder 2 dashes Lime oder Citronensaft;
3 oder 4 dashes Chartreuse (gelb);
löse dies auf mit ein wenig Wasser;
Fülle das Glas mit feinem Eis;
1½ Weinglas Kirschwasser;
mische es mit einem Barlöffel gut auf, garnire in
geschmackvoller Weise mit Weintrauben, Orange,
Ananas, Citrone, Erdbeeren; servire mit Strohhalm.

138. Orange Lemonade.
(Gebrauche ein grosses Barglas.)

1 Esslöffel Zucker;
1 dash Citronensaft;
presse 1 oder 2 Orangen hinein;
Fülle das Glas mit feinem Eis;
fülle das Glas mit Wasser, schüttele tüchtig in
einem Schüttelbecher bis sich alle Ingredientien gut
vermischt haben, garnire mit Früchten und servire
mit Strohhalm.

139. Arf and Arf.
(Gebrauche ein grosses Barglas.)

Dieses ist ein altes englisches, beliebtes, Getränk
und hat sich auch in America als Wintergetränk
grosser Beliebtheit zu erfreuen. Mische folgendes:
½ Glas Porter und fülle es auf mit Ale, (dieses ist
die englische Art.)

In diesem Lande servirt man es gewöhnlich mit
$^1/_2$ altes Ale;
$^1/_2$ neues Ale;
es ist Regel den Gast zu fragen, was für Sorten Ale
er wünscht.

140. Lemonade.
(Gebrauche ein grosses Barglas.)

$1^1/_2$ Esslöffel Zucker;
6 bis 8 dashes Citronensaft;
$^3/_4$ Glas zerschlagenes Eis;
fülle das Glas mit Wasser, schüttle es tüchtig im
Schüttelbecher, garnire mit Saisonfrucht und servire.
Um dieses Getränk gut und stark zu machen darf
man weder Zucker noch Citronensaft sparen.

141. Port Wine Sangaree.
(Gebrauche ein kleines Barglas.)

1 Theelöffel Zucker;
löse dies auf mit ein wenig Wasser;
1 oder 2 kleine Eisstücke;
1 Weinglas Portwein;
mische es gut auf mit einem Barlöffel, entferne das
Eis, wenn es verlangt wird, streue ein wenig Muscatnuss über das Getränk, und servire es.

142. Whiskey Sour.
(Gebrauche ein grosses Barglas.)

$^1/_2$ Esslöffel Zucker;
3 oder 4 dashes Citronensaft;
1 squirt Syphon Selters Wasser;
löse dieses gut auf;
Fülle das Glas mit zerschlagenem Eis;
1 Weinglas Whiskey;
mische dieses gut auf mit einem Barlöffel, seihe es
in ein Sourglas, garnire es mit kleingeschnittenen
Saisonfrüchten und servire es.

143. St. Croix Fix.
(Gebrauche ein grosses Barglas.)

$1/2$ Esslöffel feiner Zucker;
3 oder 4 dashes Citronensaft;
$1/2$ Ponyglas Ananas Syrup;
$1/2$ Weinglas Wasser;   -
löse dieses gut auf mit einem Barlöffel;
fülle das Glas mit fein geschlagenem Eis;
1 Weinglas St. Croix Rum;
mische es gut auf, und garnire es geschmackvoll
mit Weintrauben, Orange, Citrone, Ananas, Erdbeeren, und servire mit Strohhalm.

144. Porter Sangaree.
(Gebrauche ein grosses Barglas.)

$1/2$ Esslöffel feiner Zucker;
1 Weinglas Wasser;
löse dieses gut auf;
3 oder 4 kleine Eisstücke;
fülle das Glas auf mit Porter, mische es gut mit
einem Barlöffel, entferne das Eis, streue ein wenig
Muscatnuss über das Getränk und servire es.
Sei vorsichtig beim Mischen, damit der Porter
nicht über das Glas läuft.

145. Hot Lemonade.
(Gebrauche ein grosses Barglas.)

1 Esslöffel voll Zucker;
7 bis 8 dashes Citronensaft;
fülle das Glas mit heissem Wasser;
mische es gut auf mit einem Barlöffel, und servire.
Vorsichtshalber giebt man zuerst ein wenig heisses
Wasser in das Glas, damit es sich langsam erwärmt
und nicht zerspringt.

146. Brandy Scaffa.
(Gebrauche ein Sherry Weinglas)

$1/4$ Sherry-Weinglas Raspberry Syrup;
$1/4$ Sherry-Weinglas Maraschino;

PLATE No. 16.

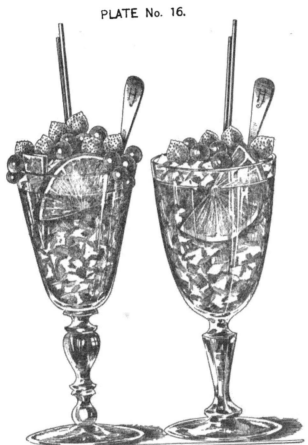

ST. CHARLES PUNCH.   BRANDY PUNCH.

¹/₄ Sherry-Weinglas Chartreuse, (grün);
¹/₄ Sherry-Weinglas Cognac;
dieses Getränk muss sehr behutsam bereitet werden,
damit sich die einzelnen Sorten Liqueure nicht vermischen, sondern schichtenweise im Glase stehen.

147. Hot Apple Toddy.

(Gebrauche ein Hot Apple Toddy Glas.)

Wenn man dieses Getränk bereitet, muss man
darauf achten, ein ziemlich grosses Glas zu wählen.
¹/₂ mittelgrosser gebackener Apfel;
¹/₂ Esslöffel voll Zucker;
löse dieses mit ein wenig heisses Wasser auf;
1 Weinglas alten Apple Jack, (Cider Brandy);
fülle das Glas auf mit heissem Wasser, mische dieses
gut auf mit einem Barlöffel, streue ein wenig Muscatnuss darüber und servire es. Wenn der Gast
es verlangt, seihe man das Getränk durch einen
Milchpunsch-Seiher. Ferner muss man darauf achten, dass nur prima Qualität Aepfel zu diesem
Getränke verwendet werden, und beim Backen
darauf sehen, dass sie schön und saftig bleiben.

148. Mulled Claret and Egg.

(Gebrauche ein grosses Barglas.)

1 Esslöffel voll Zucker;
1 Theelöffel voll Nelken und Zimmt gemischt;
1¹/₂ Weinglas Claret Wein;
giesse dieses in eine Pfanne und koche es auf;
2 frische Eidotter;
mit ein wenig Zucker zu einem leichten Teig ge-
schlagen, giesse die gekochte Flüssigkeit über den
Teig und mische rasch und tüchtig mit einem Barlöffel auf, so dass der Wein nicht zusammen läuft.
Streue ein wenig Muscatnuss darüber und servire
in einem Weinglas.

149. Californian Sherry Wine Cobbler.
(Gebrauche ein grosses Barglas.)

$^1/_2$ Esslöffel voll Zucker;
1 Ponyglas Ananas Syrup;
löse dieses gut auf mit ein wenig Wasser;
fülle das Glas mit feingeschlagenem Eis;
$1^1/_2$ Weinglas California Sherry Wein;
mische dieses gut und gründlich mit einem Barlöffel,
und garnire mit Weintrauben, Orange, Ananas, Erdbeeren in geschmackvoller Weise, übergiesse das
Ganze mit ein klein wenig ächtem Portwein, und
servire mit Strohhalm.

150. Brandy Fizz.
(Gebrauche ein grosses Barglas.)

$^1/_2$ Esslöffel voll Zucker;
3 oder 4 dashes Citronensaft;
$^3/_4$ Glas feingeschlagenes Eis;
1 Weinglas Cognac;
mische es gut mit einem Barlöffel auf, seihe in ein
Fizz oder Sourglas und fülle dasselbe mit Syphon
Vichy oder Selters Wasser, mische gut und servire.

151. Bishop.
(Gebrauche ein grosses Barglas.)

1 Esslöffel voll Zucker;
2 dashes Lime oder Citronensaft;
$^1/_2$ Weinglas Wasser;
löse dieses gut auf;
fülle das Glas mit feingeschlagenem Eis;
fülle das Glas mit Burgunder Wein und einigen
Tropfen Jamaica Rum, mische dieses gut auf mit
einem Barlöffel, garnire mit Weintrauben, Orange,
Citrone, Ananas, Erdbeeren, und servire es mit
Strohhalm.

152. Orchard Punch.
(Gebrauche ein grosses Barglas.)

2 Esslöffel voll Orchard Syrup;
2 oder 3 dashes Lime oder Citronensaft;

¹/₂ Ponyglas Ananas Syrup;
löse dieses mit ein wenig Wasser auf;
fülle das Glas mit feingeschlagenem Eis;
1 Weinglas California Cognac;
mische dieses gut auf mit einem Barlöffel, und garnire in geschmackvoller Weise mit Weintrauben,
Ananas und Orange, giesse ein wenig Portwein
darüber und servire es mit Strohhalm.

153. Gin and Tansy.
(Gebrauche ein Whiskeyglas.)

Zur Herstellung dieses Getränkes gebe man ein
kleines Büschel Tansy in eine Quartflasche und
fülle diese mit gutem Holland Gin auf, dann lasse
man dies mehrere Tage stehen, bis das Aroma des
Tansy vollständig ausgezogen ist. Beim serviren
dieses Getränkes giesse man, 1 Ponyglas präparirten
Tansy je nach der Stärke in ein Whiskeyglas und
reiche dies nebst einer Flasche Holland Gin dem
Gaste zur eigenen Bedienung. Dieses Getränk dient
als Magenbitters.

154. Jamaica Rum Sour.
(Gebrauche ein grosses Barglas)

¹/₂ Esslöffel voll Zucker;
2 oder 3 dashes Citronensaft;
1 squirt Syphon Selters Wasser;
löse dieses gut auf;
³/₄ Glas feingeschlagenes Eis;
1 Weinglas Jamaica Rum;
mische dieses mit einem Barlöffel gut auf, seihe
es in ein Sourglas, garnire mit Saisonfrüchten und
Beeren, und servire es.

155. Port Wine Flip.
(Gebrauche ein grosses Barglas.)

1 frisches Ei;
¹/₂ Esslöffel voll Zucker;
³/₄ Glas feingeschlagenes Eis;
1 Weinglas Portwein;
schüttele dieses gut auf in einem Schüttelbecher,

seihe es in ein Weinglas, streue ein wenig Muscatnuss darüber und servire.

156. Hot Arrac Punch.
(Gebrauche ein Heisswasser-Glas.)

1 oder 2 Stücke Würfelzucker;
löse gut auf mit ein wenig Wasser;
3 oder 4 Tropfen Citronensaft;
³/₄ Weinglas Arrac, (Batavia);
fülle das Glas auf mit heissem Wasser, mische es gut auf mit einem Barlöffel, streue etwas Muscatnuss darüber und servire.

157. Brandy Sangaree.
(Gebrauche ein kleines Barglas.)

1 oder 2 Eisstücke;
¹/₂ Weinglas Wasser;
¹/₂ Esslöffel voll feiner Zucker;
1 Weinglas Brandy;
mische es gut mittelst eines Barlöffels, und streue ein wenig Muscatnuss auf das Getränk, entferne das Eis wenn es verlangt wird, und servire.

158. Gin Julep.
(Gebrauche ein grosses Barglas.)

³/₄ Esslöffel voll Zucker;
3 oder 4 Zweige frische Krausemünze, (Mint);
¹/₂ Weinglas Wasser;
presse dieses mit einem Barlöffel gut aus;
fülle das Glas mit feingeschlagenem Eis;
1¹/₄ Weinglas Holland Gin;
mische dieses gut und gründlich, garnire das Getränke geschmackvoll in der Art wie Mint Julep, mit Krausemünze, die Stengel nach unten bouquetartig, und mit Saisonfrüchten. Sodann bestreue man das Ganze mit etwas fein pulversirten Zucker, giesse ein paar Tropfen Jamaica Rum darauf, und servire es mit Strohhalm.

159. Hot Scotch Whiskey Sling.
(Gebrauche ein Heisswasser-Glas.)

1 Stück Würfelzucker;
³/₄ Glas heisses Wasser;
1 Stück Citronenschale;
1 Weinglas Scotch Whiskey;
mische es gut auf mit einem Barlöffel, streue ein
wenig Muscatnuss darüber, und servire es.

160. Sherry Wine and Bitters.
(Gebrauche ein Sherry Weinglas.)

Bei Bereitung dieses Getränkes ist es nothwendig
darauf zu achten, dass niemals mehr als zwei dash
von dem Bitters angewendet wird, da sonst der
Geschmack des Sherryweines leiden würde, dagegen
aber soll der Bartender trachten, durch eine ge-
wandte Drehung des Glases zu bewirken, dass der
Bitters (Boker's genuine only), sich innen in dem
ganzen Glas vertheilt; fülle das Glas mit Sherrywein und servire es.

161. Hot Milk Punch.
(Gebrauche ein grosses Barglas.)

1 Esslöffel voll Zucker;
¹/₄ Weinglas St. Croix Rum;
³/₄ Weinglas Brandy; (wenn verlangt, Jamaica
 Rum)
fülle das Glas mit heisser Milch;
mische es gut auf mit einem Barlöffel, streue ein
wenig Muscatnuss darüber, und servire es.
Dieses Getränk darf niemals mit einem Schüttelbecher geschüttelt, sondern nur mit einem Barlöffel
gemischt werden. Im Falle der Bartender die betreffende heisse Milch nicht zur Verfügung haben
sollte, so gebrauche man etwas condensirte Milch
und fülle das Glas mit heissem Wasser.

162. Gin Cocktail.
(Gebrauche ein grosses Barglas.)

Fülle das Glas mit feingeschlagenem Eis;
2 oder 3 dashes Gum Syrup;

2 oder 3 dashes Bitters; (Boker's genuine only);
1 dash Curaçoa oder Absinthe;
1 Weinglas Holland Gin;
mische dieses mit einem Barlöffel tüchtig auf, seihe
es in ein geschmackvolles Cocktail Glas, füge ein
kleines Stück Citronenschale hinzu und servire es.

163. Tom and Jerry, (cold).
(Gebrauche ein Tom and Jerry Mug oder Glas.)

Dieses Getränk wird ganz auf dieselbe Weise
präparirt wie heisser Tom und Jerry, nur mit dem
Unterschiede dass man kaltes Wasser oder kalte
Milch verwendet.

164. Hot Whiskey.
(Gebrauche ein heisses Whiskeyglas.)

Hierbei ist die Regel zu beachten, dass der Barlöffel immer im Getränk servirt wird. Ferner muss
dem Gast stets ein Glas mit fein zerschlagenes Eis
vorgesetzt werden, damit er sich desselben zur Abkühlung des Getränkes bedienen kann. Mische wie
folgt:
1 oder 2 Stücke Würfelzucker, löse diese auf mit
etwas heissem Wasser;
1 Weinglas Scotch Whiskey;
fülle das Glas mit heissem Wasser und mische es
gut auf mit einem Barlöffel, füge ein kleines Stück
Citronenschale hinzu, streue ein wenig Muscatnuss
darauf und servire. Es ist durchweg Regel, dass man
zu diesem Getränk Scotch Whiskey verwendet, ausser
der Gast verlangt ausdrücklich eine andere Sorte.

165. Medford Rum Punch.
(Gebrauche ein grosses Barglas.)

³/₄ Esslöffel voll Zucker;
2 oder 3 dashes Citronensaft;
löse dieses gut auf mit ein wenig Wasser;
fülle das Glas mit feinem Eis;
1¹/₂ Glas Medford Rum;
mische dieses gut auf mit einem Barlöffel, garnire

in geschmackvoller Weise mit Orange, Ananas, etc.,
giesse ein paar Tropfen Jamaica Rum hinzu und
servire mit Strohhalm.

166. Whiskey Fix.
(Gebrauche ein grosses Barglas.)

1/2 Esslöffel feiner Zucker;
2 oder 3 dashes Lime oder Citronensaft;
löse dieses auf mit ein wenig Wasser;
1/2 Ponyglas Ananas Syrup;
3/4 Glas feingeschlagenes Eis;
1 Weinglas Whiskey;
mische dieses tüchtig mit einem Barlöffel, garnire in
geschmackvoller Weise, mit Orange, Ananas, Erdbeeren, etc., und servire mit Strohhalm.

167. Gin Smash.
(Gebrauche ein grosses Barglas.)

1/2 Esslöffel feiner Zucker;
2 oder 3 Zweige frische Krausemünze (Mint);
presse dieses gut mit einem Barlöffel und etwas
   Wasser;
1/2 Glas feingeschlagenes Eis;
1 Weinglas Holland Gin;
mische dieses gut auf, seihe es in ein Sourglas, garnire mit Saisonfrüchten und servire.

168. Hot Locomotive.
(Gebrauche ein grosses Barglas.)

1 frischer Eidotter;
1/2 Esslöffel feiner Zucker;
1 Ponyglas Honig;
löse dies gut auf mit einem Barlöffel;
1 1/2 Weinglas Burgunder oder Claret Wein;
1/2 Ponyglas Curaçoa;
schütte dies in ein kleines Geschirr, und stelle auf's
Feuer bis es anfängt zu kochen, dann giesse es
3 oder 4 Mal von einer Glas oder Mug zum andern,
füge eine Scheibe Citrone hinzu, streue ein wenig
Zimmt darüber und servire. Dies ist ein sehr er-
wärmendes Getränk.

169. Whiskey Fizz.

(Gebrauche ein grosses Barglas.)

$^1/_2$ Esslöffel voll Zucker;
2 oder 3 dashes Citronensaft;
löse dieses auf mit etwas Selters Wasser;
fülle das Glas mit feingeschlagenem Eis;
1 Weinglas Whiskey;
mische dieses gründlich auf mit einem Barlöffel und
seihe es in ein grosses Bar oder Fizz Glas; fülle das
Glas auf mit Syphon Selters oder Vichy Wasser,
mische gut auf und servire es.

170. Stone Wall.

(Gebrauche ein grosses Barglas.)

$^1/_4$ Esslöffel voll Zucker;
3 oder 4 Eisstücke;
1 Weinglas Whiskey;
1 Flasche plain Soda Wasser;
mische dieses gut auf mit einem Barlöffel, entferne
das Eis und servire. Dies ist ein sehr kühlendes
Getränk und wird im Sommer vielfach getrunken.

171. Hot Rum.

(Gebrauche ein Heisswasser-Glas.)

1 oder 2 Stücke Würfelzucker;
löse dieses auf mit etwas heissem Wasser;
1 Weinglas Jamaica Rum;
fülle das Glas mit heissem Wasser;
mische dieses gut auf mit einem Barlöffel und streue
ein wenig Muscatnuss darüber, und servire es. Zu
diesem Getränk verwendet man immer Jamaica
Rum, ausser wenn ausdrücklich eine anderen Sorte
Rum verlangt wird.

172. Wine Lemonade.

Gebrauche ein grosses Barglas.)

1 Esslöffel voll Zucker;
5 oder 6 dashes Citronensaft;
fülle das Glas mit feinzerschlagenem Eis;

1 Weinglas Sherry, Port oder Claret Wein, je
nach Belieben des Gastes;
fülle das Glas auf mit Wasser und schüttele dieses
tüchtig in einem Schüttelbecher, garnire das Getränk in geschmackvoller Weise mit Weintrauben,
Orange, Citrone, Ananas, Erdbeeren, und servire
mit Strohhalm. Dieses ist ein in Italien beliebtes
Getränk.

173. Hot Irish Whiskey Punch.
(Gebrauche ein Heisswasser-Glas.)

1 oder 2 Stücke Würfelzucker;
1 squirt Citronensaft;
löse dieses auf mit etwas heissem Wasser;
1 Weinglas Irish Whiskey;
fülle das Glas auf mit heissem Wasser;
füge eine Scheibe Citrone hinzu, mische dieses gut
mit dem Barlöffel, streue ein wenig Muscatnuss
darüber, und servire.

174. Stone Fence.
(Gebrauche ein kleines Barglas.)

1 Weinglas Whiskey;
2 oder 3 Eisstücke;
fülle das Glas mit gutem Apfelwein, (Cider);
mische es gut auf mit einem Barlöffel, und servire.

175. Sherry Wine Sangaree.
(Gebrauche ein Whiskeyglas.)

1 Theelöffel feiner Zucker;
löse diesen auf in etwas Wasser;
1 oder 2 Eisstücke;
1 Weinglas Sherrywein;
mische es gut auf mit einem Barlöffel, entferne das
Eis; streue ein wenig Muscatnuss darüber, und
servire.

176. Old Tom Gin Cocktail.
(Gebrauche ein grosses Barglas.)

Fülle das Glas mit feingeschlagenem Eis;
2 oder 3 dashes Gum Syrup;

1 oder 2 dashes Bitters, (Boker's genuine only);
1 oder 2 dashes Curaçoa oder Absinthe, je nach
Belieben;
1 Weinglas Old Tom Gin;
mische dieses gut auf mit einem Barlöffel und seihe
es in ein Cocktailglas, füge ein Stück Citronenschale
hinzu, und servire.

177. Gin Toddy.
(Gebrauche ein Whiskeyglas.)

$1/2$ Theelöffel voll Zucker;
löse diesen gut auf mit etwas Wasser;
1 oder 2 Eisstücke;
1 Weinglas Holland Gin;
mische dieses gut auf mit einem Barlöffel und servire. Beim Serviren dieses Getränkes an der Bar,
reiche dem Gast die Flasche mit Holland Gin, damit
er sich selbst bedienen kann.

178. Soda and Nectar.
(Gebrauche ein grosses Barglas.)

3 oder 4 dashes Citronensaft;
$3/4$ Glas Wasser;
$1/2$ kleinen Theelöffel doppeltkohlensaures Natron;
(Bicarbonate of Soda);
$1/2$ Theelöffel voll Zucker;
löse dies gut auf, und füge $1/2$ Theelöffel voll Wein-
steinsäure hinzu und servire es rasch, indem das
Getränk dadurch moussirend wird und sonst den
Effect verliert. Dieses Getränk ist sehr gut gegen
Magenbeschwerden.

179. Gin and Molasses.
(Gebrauche ein Whiskeyglas.)

Bedecke den Boden des Whiskeyglases mit etwas
Gin, dann nehme einen Esslöffel voll schwarzen
prima New Orleans Molasses, reiche dieses mit der
Flasche Holland Gin und einem kleinen zierlichen
Barlöffel dem Gaste, dass er sich selbst bedienen
kann. Die Reinigung des zu diesem Getränke

benützten Glases muss mit heissem Wasser geschehen, da sich der haftenbleibende Molasses in kaltem Wasser schwer löst.

180. Fancy Brandy Sour.
(Gebrauche ein grosses Barglas.)

$1/_2$ Esslöffel voll Zucker;
2 oder 3 dashes Citronensaft;
1 squirt Syphon Selters Wasser;
löse dieses gut auf;
fülle das Glas mit feingeschlagenem Eis;
1 Weinglas Cognac;
mische dieses tüchtig auf mit einem Barlöffel, seihe es in ein fancy Sourglas, garnire es mit kleingeschnittenen Saisonfrüchten und servire. Siehe Illustration, Tafel No. 11.

181. Port Wine Cobbler.
(Gebrauche ein grosses Barglas.)

$1/_2$ Esslöffel voll Zucker;
1 Ponyglas Orchard Syrup;
$1/_2$ Weinglas Wasser;
löse dieses gut auf;
fülle das Glas mit feingeschlagenem Eis;
$1^1/_2$ Weinglas Portwein;
mische dieses gut auf mit einem Barlöffel, garnire in geschmackvoller Weise mit Weintrauben, Orange, Ananas, Erdbeeren, Citrone, und servire es mit Strohhalm.

182. Rock and Rye Whiskey.
(Gebrauche ein Whiskeyglas.)

Dies Getränk muss vorsichtig präparirt werden, wenn es Flaschen- oder Gallonenweise bereitet wird; man beachte dabei, dass man nur den besten, reinen weissen Zuckerkand und prima Whiskey in Anwendung bringt, da es vielfach von Hals- und Brustleidenden als Medicin getrunken wird.

Beim Serviren dieses Getränks an der Bar nehme

man ein Glas mit einem halben Esslöffel voll Zuckerkand (Rock Candy) aufgelöst, und verabreiche dieses
mit der Flasche Rye Whiskey dem Gaste zur Selbstbedienung.

183. Gin Sour.
(Gebrauche ein grosses Barglas.)

½ Esslöffel Zucker;
2 oder 3 dashes Citronensaft;
1 dash Limesaft;
1 squirt Syphon Selterswasser;
löse dieses gut auf mit einem Barlöffel;
¾ Glas feingeschlagenes Eis;
1 Weinglas Holland Gin;
mische dieses gut auf, seihe es in ein Sourglas, garnire mit klein geschnittenen Saisonfrüchten und
servire es.

184. Peach and Honey.
(Gebrauche ein kleines Barglas.)

1 Esslöffel Honig;
1 Weinglas Peach Brandy (Pfirsich Cognac);
mische dieses gut auf mit einem Barlöffel und
servire.   Dies war früher ein sehr beliebtes Wintergetränk und vertrat die Stelle von Rock and Rye.

185. Sherry Wine Egg Nogg.
(Gebrauche ein grosses Barglas.)

1 frisches Ei;
½ Esslöffel Zucker;
fülle das Glas mit feingeschlagenem Eis;
1 Ponyglas Cognac;
1 Weinglas Sherrywein;
schüttele es gut in einem Schüttelbecher, seihe es in
ein fancy Barglas, streue ein wenig Muscatnuss darüber und servire.

186. Hot Brandy Sling.
(Gebrauche ein Heisswasser-Glas.)

1 Stück Würfelzucker;
löse diesen auf mit etwas heissem Wasser;

1 Weinglass Cognac;
fülle das Glas auf mit heissem Wasser, mische gut
auf mit einem Barlöffel, bestreue mit ein wenig
Muscatnuss und servire.

187. Medford Rum Smash.
(Gebrauche ein grosses Barglas.)

1/2 Esslöffel Zucker;
1/2 Weinglas Wasser;
2 oder 3 Zweige Krausemünze (Mint);
presse dies mit einem Barlöffel gut aus;
1/2 Glas feingeschlagenes Eis;
1 Weinglas Medford Rum;
mische dieses mit einem Barlöffel gut auf und seihe
es in ein Sourglas, garnire mit klein geschnittenen
Saisonfrüchten und servire.

188. Gin Fix.
(Gebrauche ein grosses Barglas.)

1/2 Esslöffel Zucker;
3 oder 4 dashes Lime oder Citronensaft;
1/2 Ponyglas Ananas Syrup;
löse dieses in etwas Wasser auf;
fülle das Glas mit feingeschlagenem Eis;
1 Weinglas Holland Gin:
mische es mit einem Barlöffel gut auf, garnire es mit
Weintrauben, Orange, Citrone, Ananas, Erdbeeren,
'n geschmackvoller Weise; servire mit Strohhalm.

189. Cold Brandy Toddy.
(Gebrauche ein Whiskeyglas.)

1/2 Theelöffel voll Zucker;
1/2 Weinglas Wasser;
löse diese gut auf;
1 oder 2 Eisstücke;
1 Weinglas Cognac;
mische dieses gut auf mit einem Barlöffel, entferne
das Eis und servire es. Es ist Regel, dass man dem
Gast die Flasche Brandy (Cognac) giebt, so dass er
sich selbst bedienen kann.

190. Gin and Wormwood.
(Gebrauche ein kleines Barglas.)

Bei Bereitung dieses Getränkes nehme man 6–8
kleine Stücke Wormwood, placire diese in eine
Quart-Flasche und fülle diese auf mit Holland Gin.
Dann lasse man dieses einige Tage stehen bis das
Aroma des Wormwood vollständig ausgezogen ist.
Beim Serviren des Getränkes giesse man ein Ponyglas Wormwood in ein Whiskeyglas und reiche
dieses nebst einer Flasche Holland Gin dem Gaste
zur eigenen Bedienung.

191. Bottle of Cocktail for Parties.
(Gebrauche eine Flasche.)

1 quart guten alten Whiskey; dass heist wenn
    die Flasche diese Quantität hält;
1 Ponyglas Curaçoa (roth);
1 Weinglas Gum Syrup;
³/₄ Ponyglas Bitters; (Boker's genuine only)
dann schüttele dieses in den Schüttelbecher mehr-
mals hin und her, dann verkorke dieselbe gut und
man wird eine gute Flasche Cocktail haben. Dieses
Getränk in Flaschen ist sehr zu empfehlen und
bequem für Reisende.

192. Claret and Champagne Cup a la Brunow.
(Gebrauche eine Punchbowle für eine Gesellschaft von 20.)

Obengenanntes excellentes Getränk war und ist
immer ein Lieblingsgetränk der russischen Monar-
chen gewesen und hat daher grosse Recommandation
in Russland. Mische folgendes:
3 Flaschen Claret;
²/₃ Pint Curaçoa;
1 Pint Sherrywein;
1 Pint Cognac;
2 Weinglas Himbeersaft;
3 Orangen, (schneide diese in Scheiben);
1 Citrone, (schneide diese in Scheiben);
Einige Zweige Balsam, oder Extract;

2 Flaschen importirtes Selters Wasser;
3 Flaschen Soda Wasser;
mische dieses gut auf mit einem Barlöffel oder Ladle
und lasse es ungefähr eine Stunde stehen, seihe es
dann in eine Bowle, schneide frische Früchte auf,
und garnire es in geschmackvoller Weise und servire es in Weingläsern.

193. Bombay Punch.
(Gebrauche eine Punschbowle.)

Reibe 6 Citronen an einer entsprechenden Quantität Zucker derart ab, dass das Gelbe der Citronenschale von der Citrone vollständig entfernt ist, dann
lege man diesen präparirten Zucker in die Bowle
und füge hinzu:
1 Pfund Würfelzucker;
2 Flaschen importirtes Selterswasser;
1 Ananas in Scheiben geschnitten;
6 Orangen in Scheiben geschnitten;
1 Box Erdbeeren;
2 Citronen in Scheiben geschnitten;
mische dies gut mit einem Löffel und nehme dazu:
4 Flaschen Champagner;
1 Flasche Cognac;
1 Flasche Pale Sherrywein;
1 Flasche Madeirawein;
1 Gill Maraschino;
mische es gut und gründlich auf mit einem Löffel
und eise die Bowle in geschmackvoller Weise nach
Vorschrift und servire es in Weingläsern.

194. Prussian Grandeur Punch.
(Gebrauche eine grosse Punschbowle.)

1½ Pfund Würfelzucker;
6 Citronen, geschnitten in Scheiben;
1 Gill Anisette;
1 Flasche Berliner Kümmel;

6 Orangen, geschnitten in Scheiben;
1 Flasche Kirschwasser;
$^1/_2$ Gallone Wasser;
6 Flaschen Nordhäuser Kornbranntwein;
1 Gill Curaçoa;
mische dieses gut auf mit einem Punschlöffel, eise
die Bowle und garnire sie geschmackvoll mit klein
geschnittenen Saisonfrüchten, nach vorgeschriebener
Weise und servire in Weingläsern.

195. Empire Punch.
(Gebrauche eine extra grosse Punchbowle.)

Reibe 4 Citronen an einer entsprechenden Quantität Stückenzucker derart ab, dass das Gelbe von der
Citrone vollständig entfernt ist; ebenso verfahre
man mit 2 Orangen.
1$^1/_2$ Pfund Stückenzucker;
1 Ananas, geschnitten in Scheiben;
12 Orangen, geschnitten in Scheiben;
1 Box Erdbeeren;
2 Flaschen Apollinariswasser;
mische gut auf mit einem grossen Löffel, füge hinzu
$^1/_2$ Gill Maraschino;
$^1/_2$ Gill Curaçoa;
$^1/_2$ Gill Benedictine;
$^1/_2$ Gill Jamaica Rum;
1 Flasche Cognac;
4 Flaschen Tokayerwein;
2 Flaschen Madeira;
4 Flaschen Chateau Lafitte;
6 Flaschen Champagner;
mische gut auf mit einem langen Punschlöffel, seihe
es durch einen feinen Seiher in eine andere Bowle
und garnire in geschmackvollster Weise mit Saisonfrüchten, wie Weintrauben, Ananas, Orange, Erdbeeren, etc., nach Vorschrift, und dieser Punsch
wird an jeder kaiser- oder königlichen Tafel einen
glänzenden Sieg erringen.

196. Hot Gin Sling.
(Gebrauche ein Heisswasser-Glas.)

1 Stück Würfelzucker;
löse dieses in ein wenig heissem Wasser gut auf;
1 Weinglas Holland Gin;
fülle das Glass mit heissem Wasser, mische es gut
mit einem Barlöffel, bestreue es mit etwas Muscatnuss und servire.

197. Brandy Daisy.
(Gebrauche ein grosses Barglas.)

$1/2$ Esslöffel voll Zucker;
2 oder 3 dashes Citronensaft;
1 squirt Selterswasser;
löse dieses gut auf mit einem Barlöffel;
$1/2$ Glas Chartreuse (gelb);
fülle das Glas mit feingeschlagenem Eis;
1 Weinglas Cognac;
mische dieses gut mit einem Barlöffel auf, placire
die Frucht in ein fancy Barglas, seihe die Ingredientien hinein und servire.

198. Japanese Cocktail.
(Gebrauche ein grosses Barglas.)

$3/4$ Glas feingeschlagenes Eis;
2 oder 3 dashes Orgeat Syrup;
2 oder 3 dashes Bitters, (Boker's genuine only);
2 dashes Maraschino;
1 Glas Eau Celeste (Himmelswasser);
mische gut mit einem Barlöffel, seihe es in ein fancy
Cocktailglas, füge ein Stück Citronenschale hinzu,
und servire es.

199. Shandy Gaff.
(Gebrauche ein grosses Barglas oder Mug.)

Fülle das Glas $1/2$ voll Old Ale oder Bass Ale und
die andere Hälfte mit Belfast Ginger Ale; mische
gut auf mit einem Barlöffel und servire es.

200. Saratoga Cocktail.
(Gebrauche ein grosses Barglas.)

³/₄ Glas feingeschlagenes Eis;
2 oder 3 dashes Ananas Syrup;
2 oder 3 dashes Bitters, (Boker's genuine only);
2 oder 3 dashes Maraschino (di Zara));
³/₄ Glas guten alten Cognac;
mische dieses mit einem Barlöffel, placire 2 oder 3
Erdbeeren in ein fancy Cocktailglas, seihe es und
füge ein Stück Citronenschale und 1 squirt Champagner hinzu und servire es.

201. How to serve a Ponyglas of Brandy.
(Gebrauche ein Pony Glas.)

Beim Serviren dieses Getränks giesse man ein
Ponyglas Cognac in ein gewöhnliches Whiskeyglas,
worin einige kleine Stückchen Eis gelegt sind, und
servire solches mit einem Glas Eiswasser.

202. Black Stripe.
(Gebrauche ein grosses Barglas.)

1 Weinglas St. Croix Rum;
¹/₂ Esslöffel voll Molasses;
Dieses Getränk kann zu jeder Jahreszeit genossen
werden, jedoch mit dem Unterschiede, dass man im
Winter das Glas mit warmem Wasser füllt, während
man sich im Sommer des Eises bedient. Bestreue
mit Muscatnuss und servire.

203. Soldiers Camping Punch.

Koche einen grossen Kessel schwarzen, starken
Caffee, dann nehme eine grosse Blechschüssel, lege
4 Pfund Würfelzucker in dieselbe, giesse 4 Flaschen
Cognac und 2 Flaschen Jamaica Rum darüber, zünde
dies an, lasse den Zucker gut auflösen, giesse die
Flüssigkeit langsam in den Caffee und mische diesen
gut auf. Dieses Getränk ist sehr zu empfehlen für
Soldaten im Bivouac, oder auch Reisenden, indem es
einfach zu bereiten und sehr erwärmend ist.

204. Gin and Calamus.
(Gebrauche ein Whiskeyglas)

Man nehme zur Bereitung dieses Getränks 3 oder
4 lange Wurzeln Calmus, placire diese in eine Quart-
flasche und fülle mit Holland Gin auf, dann lasse
einige Tage stehen, bis das Aroma des Calmus vollständig ausgezogen ist. Beim Serviren giesse man
ein Ponyglas des präparirten Calmus in ein Whiskeyglas und reiche dieses nebst einer Flasche Holland
Gin dem Gaste zur eigenen Bedienung.

205. Orgeat Lemonade.
(Gebrauche ein grosses Barglas.)

$1^1/_2$ Weinglas Orgeat Syrup;
$1/_2$ Esslöffel Zucker;
7 oder 8 dashes Citronensaft;
$^3/_4$ Glas zerschlagenes Eis;
fülle das Glas mit Wasser;
mische es gut auf, und garnire es geschmackvoll
mit Weintrauben, Orange, Citrone, Ananas, Erdbeeren, und servire mit Strohhalm.

Dies ist ein sehr kühlender Trank und in warmer
Jahreszeit sehr beliebt.

206. Beef Tea.
(Gebrauche ein Heisswasser-Glas.)

$1/_4$ Theelöffel Beef-Extract;
fülle das Glas mit heissem Wasser;
mische es gut auf mit einem Barlöffel, und servire
dies nebst Salz; Pfeffer und Celerysalz, dass sich der
Gast selbst damit bedienen kann. Auf Wunsch füge
man etwas Sherrywein oder Cognac hinzu.

207. Gin and Milk.
(Gebrauche ein Whiskeyglas.)

Reiche das Glas nebst der Flasche Holland Gin
dem Gaste, damit derselbe die Quantität Gin nach
Geschmack wähle, fülle dann das Glas auf mit guter,
eiskalter Milch, mische dieses gut mit einem Barlöffel auf und servire.

208. Columbia Skin.
(Gebrauche ein kleines Barglas.)

1 Theelöffel voll Zucker;
löse diesen mit ein wenig Wasser auf;
1 Schnitte Citrone;
2 oder 3 Eisstücke;
1 Weinglas Rum;
mische es gut auf mit einem Barlöffel, streue ein wenig Muscatnuss darüber und servire. Das Getränk wird hauptsächlich in Boston und Umgegend unter diesen Namen getrunken.

209. Brandy Straight.
(Gebrauche ein Whiskeyglas.)

Reiche das Glas nebst der Flasche Cognac dem Gast, damit er sich selbst bedienen kann. Sollte der Cognac, der in der Regel nicht auf Eis gestellt wird, nicht kalt genug sein, so hat der Bartender einige Stücke Eis beizufügen.

210. Claret Cobbler.
(Gebrauche ein grosses Barglas oder Goblet.)

1 Esslöffel voll Orchard Syrup;
$^1/_2$ Esslöffel feiner Zucker;
$^1/_4$ Orange;
1 squirt Syphon Selterswasser;
löse dieses gut auf mit einem Barlöffel;
fülle das Glas mit fein geschlagenem Eis;
$1^1/_2$ Weinglas guten Claret Wein;
mische gut und garnire mit Scheiben Orange, Ananas, Citrone, etc., und servire.

211. Milk and Selters.
(Gebrauche ein grosses Barglas.)

Beim Serviren dieses Getränks, welches ein Temperenzgetränk ist, wird auf folgende Art und Weise verfahren: Man fülle das Glas bis zur Hälfte mit Syphon Selters oder Vichy Wasser und dann fülle

man es auf mit guter frischer Milch; würde man es
auf umgekehrte Weise füllen, erhielte man nichts
als Schaum im Glase, was sehr unangenehm und
zeitraubend für den Bartender sein würde.

212. Whiskey and Cider.
(Gebrauche ein Whiskeyglas.)

Reiche das Glas nebst der Flasche Whiskey dem
Gast zur Selbstbedienung und fülle dann das Glas
auf mit gutem Apfelwein (Cider). Hierbei ist zu
empfehlen, nur guten Apfelwein zu gebrauchen, da
künstlicher Cider das Getränk nur verderben würde.

213. Champagne Velvet.
(Gebrauche einen grossen Goblet.)

Dieses Getränk wird nur bereitet wenn die Gäste
eine kleine oder grosse Flasche Champagner und
eine Flasche Guinness Stout zu öffnen beabsichtigen.
Dann mische man wie folgt:
fülle den Goblet $1/2$ voll mit Porter;
dann fülle das übrige mit Champagner;
mische vorsichtig mit einem Barlöffel und servire.
Champagner Velvet ist zwar ein kostspieliges aber
dafür auch ein sehr wohlschmeckendes Getränk.

214. Burnt Brandy and Peach.
(Gebrauche ein kleines Barglas.)

Dieses ist ein sehr populäres Getränk in den süd-
lichen Staaten Americas und wird gegen Diarrhoe
wirksam angewendet.
1 Weinglas Cognac;
$1/2$ Esslöffel voll Zucker;
Man brenne dieses in einer Pfanne braun;
2 oder 3 Scheiben getrocknete Pfirsiche;
placire diese in ein Whiskeyglas und füge den ge-
brannten Zucker und den Cognac hinzu; mische gut
mit einem Barlöffel, streue ziemlich viel Muscatnuss
darüber und servire.

TO THE READER.

The reader's special attention is called to the perusal of the remaining pages of this book. They contain the business announcements of a few first-class, and in every respect reliable purveyors to our trade. The author does not base his recommendation an hearsay or on casual acquaintance, but on his business connections with the several firms for a long number of years. The purchase of supplies is an important factor in any business, but in none more so than in ours. No man can build up a good trade or gain a reputation in the Saloon or Bar business, unless he obtains his supplies from first-class houses that will furnish him with the best the market affords. To enable the reader to do this, the following pages were added to complete this book.

HARRY JOHNSON,

Author.

GEORGE EHRET'S
— FAMOUS —
Extra Lager Beer.

*T*O the bartender it is a matter of the greatest importance which Bitters he should use in the
preparation of mixed drinks, of which they are one
of the principal flavor-giving ingredients. The only
advice the author of this book can give, is: "Always
use the very best that money can procure."

The unmistakable results of observation and
experience during the last 60 years have led to the
popular verdict that BOKER'S BITTERS, first in-
troduced into this country in 1828, and manu-
factured here by an improved process since 1849,
are now justly celebrated as one of those productions,
in which the United States excel all the rest of the
World, and that they are the **MOST CONSUMMATE
HARMONY OF PALATABLE AND INVIGORATING INGREDIENTS.**

BOKER'S BITTERS are not only a remarkably
fine Cordial, if taken **PURE,** but are unequalled for
mixing with other Cordials, such as Curacoa, Anisette, Kümmel, Vermouth, Wines or Liquors, as
well as for the preparation of the refined drinks
of the bar.

HARRY JOHNSON.

Roosevelt Cigar Factory.

PETER · FRENSEN,

MANUFACTURER OF

FINE CIGARS

175 SOUTH & 137 ROOSEVELT STS.,

NEW YORK.

This factory was successfully carried on for 13 years at No. 492 Third Avenue, and for the last five years with largely increased facilities at the corner of Roosevelt and South Streets. An experience of 27 years in this country enabled me to study the wants of the public, and furnish my customers with goods that will give entire satisfaction.

Harry Johnson sold over 70,000 of my cigars at retail over his counter in a single year. The proprietors of other prominent hotels and bar-rooms will cheerfully testify that the cigars I furnished them gave satisfaction to their customers and increased their trade.

ALES and PORTERS.

The American people are rapidly approaching the English and Germans in their love for and consumption of Malt Liquors. With this increasing consumption comes a constantly growing critical taste as to the quality of the goods purchased. While in Lager brilliancy at a low temperature is the principal requisite, we must look to the Ales and Porters for the more delicate flavors to be secured by the skillful manipulation of Malt and Hops, and for those nourishing and greatly stimulating qualities so often sought by physicians, and so acceptable and beneficial to all lovers of Malt Liquors.

As a matter of course every good Ale will have its admirers, and it might seem difficult to discriminate between the different brands. But as I have often been asked, as the result of my 30 years' experience in the business, whose Ale I had found the most satisfactory, I have no hesitation in saying here that for uniform good quality and for all the excellences to be found in well-brewed Malt and Hops, The fresh and stock Ales and Porters produced by

Mess. W. A. MILES & CO.,

at the *Croton Brewery, 55, 57 & 59 Chrystie St.,* are superior to any similar goods in the market.

In the bottling of their Ales they have the rare advantage of selections from a large stock, and their SUPER CROTON has for years been acknowledged in every respect to equal the famous Scotch Brands fr Glasgow and Edinburgh, while their PALE INDIA is equally as good and often better than Be put upon our market.

A fair trial of their goods I am confid this opinion of them.

HAR

MY REMARKS ON WHISKEY.

During the last 30 years that I have been connected actively in the Hotel and Liquor business, I
have heard a great number of arguments and dis-
putes concerning whiskey the national beverage of
our country. I have come to the conclusion, after
trying numerous kinds, that the

"TIDAL WAVE". & "VICTOR" BRANDS

—: OF :—

THE HANNIS DISTILLING CO.,

are the leading brands and by far superior to all
others, not alone in their acknowledged uniformity
and smoothness for drinking purposes, but also in
their adaptability for mixing and compounding
drinks of the present day. These conclusions have
not been drawn from opinions, but are based on solid
foundations and facts, as the greatest success I ever
achieved was in my last venture, when I handled and
used these goods exclusively for a number of years,
and in all that period I never heard a complaint or
word of dissatisfaction from my numerous customers.
As whiskey to=day is the chief article sold in our
line of business, it would be well for those in our
trade to call on Mr. Theo. Bomeisler, the general
agent of the "Tidal Wave" and "Victor" brands,
at 50 Beaver Street, New York, where I can gua-
rantee from my own experience they will be well
treated socially, and from a business point of view
will only be forwarding their own interests.

HARRY JOHNSON.

Printed in the USA
CPSIA information can be obtained
at www.ICGtesting.com
LVHW091918051023
760266LV00001B/3

9 781166 233327